ROMEO AND JULIET

WILLIAM SHAKESPEARE

Edited by Jeannie Heppell
Head of English, Queen Margaret's School, Escrick, York

Henderson Study System devised by Jeannie Heppell
© Celandine International 1995
All rights reserved

HENDERSON
PUBLISHING PLC
©1995 HENDERSON PUBLISHING PLC

HOW TO USE THIS TEXT

On the next page you will find a list of major themes contained in this text. They are in different colours. By following the instructions below, you will form a coding system which will give you immediate access to the material you will need to study the themes.

At the back of the text you will find sheets of stickers. These correspond with coloured markers at the right-hand edge of the pages. Peel off the sticker and place it exactly in position, over the matching colour guide. Fold the tab along the half-colour line, and stick down the white half to the back of the page. This allows matching colour tabs to protrude over the edge of the pages, all in line, throughout your book, making it easy to locate the material to study your theme. The references you will need for the theme will be underlined in the appropriate colour on the pages of text.

You will find that:

- **THEMES ARE <u>HIGHLIGHTED</u>**

- **QUOTATIONS ARE IMMEDIATELY ACCESSIBLE**

- **YOU HAVE INSTANT RECOGNITION OF DOMINANT THEMES**

- **YOU CAN SEE AT A GLANCE THE DOMINANT IMAGES**

- **MATERIAL FOR ESSAYS IS READILY AVAILABLE FOR YOU TO RESPOND TO INDIVIDUALLY, AVOIDING PREPARED PLANS**

- **YOUR REVISION IS ALREADY STRUCTURED**

N.B. The numbering on this text is actual, overriding split-verse lines.

Major Themes In This Text

ENMITY

LOVE

EXPEDIENCE IN LOVE

BAWDY SEX

PARENTS AND CHILDREN

PREMONITION

CHANCE/FATE

IRONY

AGE

PUNS/ANTITHESIS

LIGHT-DARK IMAGE

GUNPOWDER IMAGE

LIGHTNING IMAGE

LOVE AS A RELIGION

DEATH AS A LOVER

ROMEO AND JULIET: THE THEMES AND FEATURES

The most obvious theme in the play is ENMITY. It deals with the long-standing feud between the two foremost families of Verona, the Capulets and the Montagues. It is sharply contrasted with the theme of LOVE, the passionate relationship involving the Capulet daughter and the Montague son. It is through the tragic outcome of this love that the enmity between the families is finally resolved.

Throughout the play one theme is constantly off-set by another, YOUTH and AGE, for example. The spirit of youth pervades the text and AGE is coded for you. The patience and wisdom of age sees the folly of hot-blooded action as displayed by the group of volatile young men. The calm philosophy of Friar Lawrence is contrasted with the precipitous emotions of Romeo. The arbitrariness of the PARENT towards the CHILD in the Capulet family is balanced against the worry of the Montagues over the behaviour of their son. The idealised concept of LOVE as seen in Romeo's speeches, is set against the BAWDY obscenities which preoccupy his peer group, who only see love in terms of the sexual act, and, if they are to be believed, in as volatile a way as their quarrelling! This could also be applied to the earthy preoccupations of the Nurse. Against this is the EXPEDIENCE of allying wealth to wealth in the proposed marriage of Paris to Juliet and Benvolio's practical, if rather unromantic suggestion to the lovelorn Romeo that there are plenty more fish in the sea and he is to forget Rosaline.

This element of contrast is developed throughout the structure of the play, where for example, the poignant tenderness of the marriage scene is swiftly followed by the violence of Mercutio's death and the fatal struggle between Romeo and Tybalt. This structural device is used again when we, the audience, are anguishing on behalf of Juliet as she visualises the possible consequences of Friar Lawrence's potion and the next minute we are identifying with the bustle and mayhem in the kitchen where Capulet is driving his servants to distraction, and the Nurse to open rudeness, as he interferes with the preparations for the wedding feast. The scene which immediately follows the putative death of Juliet contains the humour of the ill-done-by musicians.

We have a reflection of this balance of opposites in the way the language abounds in the use of ANTITHESIS. This is coded with PUNS and will guide you through the difficult area of the word games used by the boys as yet another arena in which to compete with one another. The device is used in other areas too, even in moments of highest tension and tragedy; its use is a particular hallmark of the play.

A further feature which is notable is the use of the SONNET form, most evident in the first half of the play when the emphasis is on LOVE. The opening Chorus is a complete sonnet, as is the Chorus to Act 11. Parts of sonnets appear in the language of Romeo, when he is playing the part of the Petrarchan Lover to Rosaline and especially when he is conversing with Juliet and his emotion is true. All these areas have been noted for you in the margin. It is also worth noting the contrast in Juliet's approach to the language of love. She is eminently practical against his lyricism.

The tragedy which overtakes these young people is claimed to be preordained. They are 'star-crossed' states the Chorus to Act 1. What does this mean? Is it that their fate is already determined by a higher power in the Heavens, is it that the choices they make are rash, or that they are just downright unlucky? The theme which incorporates the references is CHANCE/FATE. The first, Chance, is accident, the sort of accident that incarcerates Friar John, suspected of carrying the plague, and prevents him from delivering the crucial message to Romeo, the sort of random chance that puts Romeo in the way of the illiterate servant and makes him aware of the Capulet guest list, the horrifying coincidence that Paris should choose to pay his respects to the dead at the same moment that Romeo arrives. Inauspicious stars are something else; if we believe in these then we believe in the presence of a destructive malignity which 'arranges' all these incidents to bring about the tragic end. Once you have studied the references you should decide for yourself which stance you will take. The prevailing atmosphere in 'Romeo and Juliet' is one of irrepressible youth, of passionate intensity in relationships, of precious innocence sacrificed; to which bad luck, or the inexorable plan of a malign influence add their sinister turn.

To return to the theme of ENMITY. The origin of the 'ancient grudge' is elusive! The feud seems to be of such long standing that even the perpetrators appears to have forgotten the reasons for the hostility. Old Capulet is seen to be uneasy about its prolongation at the opening: "'tis not hard, I think/For men so old as we to keep the peace", and he is determined that his nephew, Tybalt, should recognise Romeo's qualities even though the young gate-crasher is the son of his enemy. It is the young men, indeed, who fuel the injuries between the families. They thrive on the verbal cut and thrust of the contest as well as the display of skills in the actual swordplay. Mercutio involves himself despite the fact that he belongs to neither house.

He also is seduced by the element of danger in these thrilling, but ultimately fatal, games.

One of the most important aspects of the play is the use of LIGHT/DARK, not only to add authenticity to the settings, but to underline the tragic content. The two young lovers are only able to be together in the dark but the beauty of their love and their innocence radiantly illuminates these scenes. The darkness of their fate hangs over them nevertheless, and it is worth noting how many times lights are called for throughout the play; it is as if Capulet himself has an intuition that dark forces are at work!

There are many more features for you to explore. Some of the recurrent images are coded for you but you could go further and study the MILITARY metaphors, love as a DISEASE, the ARROW image, particularly with its connection with Cupid. These are located for you in your text.

There are several other themes which are highlighted for you which have not been dealt with in this introduction, but are well worth pursuing. 'Romeo and Juliet' is a delightful play and you should enjoy studying it. The treatment, using this study system, will help you to do that successfully and with confidence.

ABOUT JEANNIE HEPPELL

Jeannie Heppell is an Honours graduate of Nottingham University. She has been Head of English at Queen Margaret's School, Escrick Park, for the past twelve years and was formerly an 'A' level examiner for the Oxford Board. Previous to this, she was Deputy Director of Theatre at Ampleforth College where she devised a version of this system in order to have swift access to specific areas of play scripts. The system adapted well to the preparation of texts for examination and has been used with outstanding success by her students for over a decade at both Advanced and GCSE levels. She lives in Yorkshire with her husband and is particularly fond of West Highland terriers.

ROMEO AND JULIET

PERSONS REPRESENTED

ESCALUS, *Prince of Verona.*

PARIS, *a Young Nobleman, Kinsman to the Prince.*

MONTAGUE,
CAPULET, } *Heads of two Houses at variance with each other.*

AN OLD MAN, *Uncle to* CAPULET.

ROMEO, *Son to* MONTAGUE.

MERCUTIO, *Kinsman to the Prince, and Friend to* ROMEO.

BENVOLIO, *Nephew to* MONTAGUE, *and Friend to* ROMEO.

TYBALT, *Nephew to* LADY CAPULET.

FRIAR LAWRENCE, *a Franciscan.*

FRIAR JOHN, *of the same Order.*

BALTHASAR, *Servant to* ROMEO.

SAMPSON,
GREGORY, } *Servants to* CAPULET

PETER, *Servant to* JULIET'S Nurse.

ABRAHAM, *Servant to* MONTAGUE

An Apothecary.

Three Musicians.

Chorus.

Page *to* PARIS; *another* Page.

An Officer.

LADY MONTAGUE, *Wife to* MONTAGUE.

LADY CAPULET, *Wife to* CAPULET.

JULIET, *Daughter to* CAPULET.

Nurse to JULIET.

Citizens of *Verona; several* Men *and* Women, *relations to both Houses;*
Maskers, Guards, Watchmen, *and* Attendants.

SCENE, – *During the greater part of the play in* VERONA; *once, in the Fifth Act, at* MANTUA.

PROLOGUE

Two households, both [1] alike in dignity,
    In fair Verona, where we lay our scene,
From [2] ancient grudge break to new [3] mutiny,
    Where [4] civil blood makes civil hands unclean.
From forth the fatal loins of these two foes
    A pair of [5] star-cross'd lovers take their life:
Whose [6] misadventur'd piteous overthrows
    Do with their death bury their [7] parents' strife.
The fearful [8] passage of their death-mark'd love,
    And the continuance of their parents' rage,
Which but their children's end naught could remove,
    Is now the [9] two hours' traffic of our stage;
The which, if you with patient ears attend,
    [10] What here shall miss, our toil shall strive to mend.

ACT ONE, SCENE ONE

A PUBLIC PLACE.

Enter SAMPSON *and* GREGORY, *armed with swords and* [11] *bucklers.*

SAMPSON Gregory, o' my word, we'll not [12] carry coals.
GREGORY No, for then we should be [13] colliers.
SAMPSON I mean, [14] an we be in choler we'll draw.
GREGORY Ay, while you live, [15] draw your neck out o' the collar.
SAMPSON I strike quickly, being [16] moved.   5
GREGORY But thou art not quickly [17] moved to strike.
SAMPSON A dog of the house of Montague moves me.
GREGORY To move is to stir; and to be valiant is to stand: therefore,
    if thou art [18] moved, thou runn'st away.
SAMPSON A dog of that house shall move me to stand: [19] I will take the   10
    wall of any man or maid of Montague's.
GREGORY That shows thee a weak slave; for the [20] weakest goes to
    the wall.
SAMPSON True; and therefore women, being the weaker vessels, are ever
    thrust to the wall: therefore I will push Montague's men from the   15
    wall and [21] thrust his maids to the wall.
GREGORY The quarrel is between our masters and us their men.
SAMPSON 'Tis all one, I will show myself a tyrant: when I have fought
    with the men I will be cruel with the maids, and cut off their
    [22] heads.   20

1 equal
2 the reason for the enmity is not explained
3 street-fighting, disturbance
4 there is civil war between the families
5 destined to come to grief
6 unlucky, pitiful accidents
7 the feud
8 course
9 the play actually takes longer than two hours
10 In general terms this means that whatever the play shall lack, the actors will try to make up for.
11 shields
12 will not take an insult, like a low person, a collier, would
13 those who handle coal (a term of abuse)
14 if we are made angry we will draw our swords (to fight) Sampson is punning on the two words
15 make sure that your neck is kept out of a hangman's rope (collar) - another pun
16 motivated to anger
17 compelled to attack
18 a third meaning of moved - further puns
19 i.e. push them into the dirt (by walking nearest the wall and taking the clean side of the pavement)
20 a proverb which suggests that the woman being the weaker, should keep by the wall
21 a sexual inference, ironic in that the two sides seem to want each other's women
22 take their maidenheads (virginity) He is punning on the two meanings of the word

GREGORY The heads of the maids?

SAMPSON Ay, the heads of the maids, or their maidenheads; take it in what (1) sense thou wilt.

GREGORY They must take it in sense that feel it.

SAMPSON Me they shall feel while I am able (2) to stand: and 'tis known I am a pretty piece of flesh.   **25**

GREGORY 'Tis well thou art not fish; if thou hadst, thou hadst been (3) poor-John. – Draw thy tool; here comes two of the house of the Montagues.

     30

Enter ABRAHAM *and* Serving Man.

SAMPSON My (4) naked weapon is out: quarrel, I will back thee.

GREGORY How! turn thy (5) back and run?

SAMPSON (6) Fear me not.

GREGORY No, (7) marry; I fear thee!   **35**

SAMPSON (8) Let us take the law on our sides; let them begin.

GREGORY I will frown as I pass by; and let them take it as they (9) list.

SAMPSON Nay, as they dare. I will (10) bite my thumb at them; which is a disgrace to them if they bear it.

ABRAHAM Do you bite your thumb at us, sir?

SAMPSON I do bite my thumb, sir.

ABRAHAM Do you bite your thumb at us, sir?   **40**

SAMPSON Is the law of our side if I say ay?

GREGORY No.

SAMPSON (11) No, sir, I do not bite my thumb at you, sir; but I bite my thumb, sir.

GREGORY Do you quarrel, sir?   **45**

ABRAHAM Quarrel, sir! no, sir.

SAMPSON If you do, sir, I am for you: I serve as good a man as you.

ABRAHAM No better.

SAMPSON Well, sir.

GREGORY Say better: here comes one of my master's kinsmen.   **50**

SAMPSON Yes, better, sir.

ABRAHAM You lie.

SAMPSON Draw, if you be men. – Gregory, remember thy (12) swashing blow.   *(They fight.*

Enter BENVOLIO.

BENVOLIO Part, fools! put up your swords; you know not what you do.
     (Beats down their swords.

---

1 a pun on sense (what meaning you will, on what feeling you will)

2 a sexual inference

3 dried hake

4 his sword is out of its sheath, ready to fight

5 pun - he is teasing Sampson that he is a coward - Sampson meant that he would pick a quarrel and carry it through

6 doubt me not - Gregory picks up the other meaning and puns on it below: "I fear thee"

7 an oath, swearing by the Virgin Mary

8 Sampson suggests that they must be right by the law - it is ironic because they are starting to quarrel and are in the wrong by communicating hostility

9 want

10 biting a thumb was an insulting gesture

11 Sampson is still wary of the law and lies about his actual intentions. The petty reasons for quarrelling can be seen in the following lines

12 slashing

Enter TYBALT.   55

TYBALT What, art thou drawn among these (1) heartless hinds?
    Turn thee, Benvolio, look upon thy death.
BENVOLIO I do but keep the peace: put up thy sword,
    Or manage it to part these men with me.
TYBALT (2) What, drawn, and talk of peace! I hate the word   60
    As I hate hell, all Montagues, and thee:
    Have at thee, coward!   *(They fight.*

Enter several of both Houses, who join the fray;
then enter Citizens *with clubs.*

1 CITIZEN Clubs, (3) bills, and partisans! strike! beat them down!
    (4) Down with the Capulets! Down with the Montagues!

Enter CAPULET *in his gown, and* LADY CAPULET.

CAPULET What noise is this? – Give me my long sword, ho!   65
LADY CAPULET (5) A crutch, a crutch! – Why call you for a sword?
CAPULET My sword, I say! – Old Montague is come,
    And flourishes his blade (6) in spite of me.

Enter MONTAGUE *and* LADY MONTAGUE.

MONTAGUE Thou villain Capulet! – (7) Hold me not, let me go.
LADY MONTAGUE (8) Thou shalt not stir a foot to seek a foe.   70

Enter PRINCE, *with* Attendants.

PRINCE Rebellious subjects, enemies to peace,
    Profaners of this (9) neighbour-stained steel, –
    Will they not hear? – What, ho! you men, you beasts,
    That quench the fire of your pernicious rage
    With (10) purple fountains issuing from your veins, –   75
    On pain of torture, from those bloody hands,
    Throw your (11) mistemper'd weapons to the ground,
    And hear the sentence of your moved prince. –
    Three civil brawls, bred of an (12) airy word,
    By thee, old Capulet and Montague,   80
    Have thrice disturb'd the quiet of our streets;
    And made Verona's ancient citizens
    Cast by their grave (13) beseeming ornaments,
    To wield old (14) partisans in hands as old,
    (15) Canker'd with peace, to part your canker'd hate: 85
    If ever you disturb our streets again,

1 Pun - servants (hinds) lacking stout hearts/female deer without their stags

2 Tybalt on his entry, immediately changes the tone and increases the feeling of danger. His reason for fighting is hatred.

3 pike-like weapons

4 the citizens dislike this feud intensely

5 Lady Capulet suggests that at his age a crutch would be more suitable than a sword. She is much younger than he is

6 to scorn me

7 Capulet is preventing him from entering the fray; a possible sign that the feud is on the wane.

8 Lady Montague is much more determined than the sarcastic Lady Capulet

9 Your swords are stained with the blood of your neighbours.

10 of blood

11 Pun - they are made for an evil purpose and are also used in bad-temper.

12 trivial

13 Suitable (beseeming) because they are not weapons; "old people should not be forced to act in this way because of your enmity", is the prince's inference.

14 pikes, weapons

15 Pun 1. rusty, 2. malignant

Your lives shall pay the *(1)* forfeit of the peace.
For this time, all the rest depart away:–
You, Capulet, shall go along with me; –
And, Montague, come you this afternoon,   90
To know our further pleasure in this case,
To old *(2)* Free-town, our common judgment-place. –
Once more, on pain of death, all men depart.
          (Exeunt PRINCE *and* Attendants; CAPULET, LADY CAPULET,
                    TYBALT, Citizens, *and* Servants.

MONTAGUE *(3)* Who set this ancient quarrel new abroach? –
     Speak, nephew, were you by when it began?   95
BENVOLIO Here were the servants of your adversary
     And yours close fighting ere I did approach:
     I drew to part them: in the instant came
     The fiery Tybalt, with his sword prepar'd;
     Which, as he breath'd defiance to my ears,   100
     He swung about his head, and cut the winds,
     Who, nothing hurt withal, *(4)* hiss'd him in scorn:
     While we were interchanging thrusts and blows,
     Came more and more, and fought on part and part,
     Till the prince came, who parted *(5)* either part.   105
LADY MONTAGUE O, where is Romeo? – saw you him to-day? –
     (6) Right glad I am he was not at this fray.
BENVOLIO Madam, *(7)* an hour before the worshipp'd sun
     Peer'd forth the golden window of the east,
     A troubled mind *(8)* drave me to walk abroad;   110
     Where, – underneath the grove of *(9)* sycamore
     That westward rooteth from the city's side, –
     So early walking did I see your son:
     Towards him I made; but he was *(10)* ware of me,
     And stole into the *(11)* covert of the wood: 115
     I, measuring his affections by my own, –
     That most are busied when they're most alone, –
     Pursu'd my *(12)* humour, not pursuing his,
     And gladly shunn'd who gladly fled from me.
MONTAGUE Many a morning hath he there been seen,   120
     With tears *(13)* augmenting the fresh morning's dew,
     (14) Adding to clouds more clouds with his deep sighs:
     But all so soon as the all-cheering sun
     Should in the furthest east begin to draw
     The shady curtains from *(15)* Aurora's bed,   125
     (16) Away from light stears home my *(17)* heavy son,

1	you will be executed
2	Villa Franca, the Capulet's Castle
3	Who started this quarrel off again?
4	Benvolio dislikes Tybalt's flamboyance in his swordplay and suggests that he is an inferior fighter. Mercutio contradicts this account later
5	both sides, people from both families (only the Prince had the authority to do this)
6	Lady Montague is protective of Romeo
7	N.B. the change in the language with the change of subject matter; the bawdy, sexual innuendo has been replaced by the Petrarchan style of love poetry
8	drove
9	associated with melancholy lovers
10	wary
11	secret depths (Romeo is behaving like a text book "lover". He is imagining that he is in love with the unattainable Rosaline.)
12	mood
13	increasing
14	the clouds of mist from lovers' sighs is a motif throughout the play
15	the goddess of the dawn
16	We are introduced to the pervading theme of LIGHT/DARK here. Romeo, as the unrequited lover, hides away from the light.
17	further contrast of LIGHT/DARK

And private in his chamber *(1)* pens himself;
Shuts up his windows, locks fair daylight out,
And makes himself an artificial night:
(2) Black and portentous must his *(3)* humour prove.   130
Unless good counsel may the cause remove.
BENVOLIO My noble uncle, do you know the cause?
MONTAGUE I neither know it nor can learn of him.
BENVOLIO Have you *(4)* importun'd him by any means?
MONTAGUE Both by myself and many other friends.   135
 But he, *(5)* his own affections' counsellor,
 Is to himself, – I will not say how true, –
 But to himself so secret and so close,
 So far from *(6)* sounding and discovery,
 (7) As is the bud bit with an envious worm   140
 Ere he can spread his sweet leaves to the air,
 Or dedicate his beauty to the sun.
 Could we but learn from whence his sorrows grow,
 We would as willingly give cure as know.
BENVOLIO See where he comes: so please you, step aside;   145
 (8) I'll know his grievance or be much denied.
MONTAGUE I would thou wert so happy by thy stay
 To hear true *(9)* shrift. – Come, madam, let's away.
      (Exeunt MONTAGUE *and* LADY.

Enter ROMEO
BENVOLIO Good-morrow, cousin.
ROMEO   Is the day so young?   150
BENVOLIO But *(10)* new struck nine.
ROMEO   Ay me! sad hours seem long.
 Was that my father that went hence so fast?
BENVOLIO It was. – What sadness lengthens Romeo's hours?
ROMEO Not having that which, having, makes them short.   155
BENVOLIO In love?
ROMEO Out, –
BENVOLIO Of love?
ROMEO Out of her favour where I am in love.
BENVOLIO Alas, that love, so *(11)* gentle in his view,   160
 Should be so tyrannous and rough in proof!
ROMEO Alas, that love, *(12)* whose view is muffled still,
 Should, without eyes, see pathways to his will! –
 Where shall we dine? – O me! – *(13)* What fray was here?
 Yet tell me not, for I have heard it all.   165

1 shuts himself in

2 a premonition of the evil
 to come

3 this is more than a mood,
 it is a condition of his
 spirit

4 questioned

5 He is following the
 conventions of the
 romantic lover

6 ascertaining the depth

7 he is like a bud affected
 by a canker (worm)
 (It could be referring to
 Romeo's inner sorrow
 that his love is not
 returned)

8 I am going to find out
 what is wrong with him.

9 confession (of his ills)

10 just

11 i.e. Cupid whose
 appearance is childlike

12 Cupid is blind, but will
 find ways to bring about
 what he wants.

13 Romeo has been so lost
 in his self inflicted
 misery that he has only
 just noticed further
 evidence of the feud.

Here's much to do with hate, but *(1)* more with love: –
Why, then, O *(2)* brawling love! O loving hate!
O *(3)* anything, of nothing first create!
O heavy lightness! serious *(4)* vanity!
Mis-shapen chaos of well-seeming forms!   170
Feather of lead, bright smoke, cold fire, sick health!
(5) Still-waking sleep, that is not what it is! –
(6) This love feel I, that feel no love in this.
Dost thou not laugh?

BENVOLIO   No, *(7)* coz, I rather weep.   175

ROMEO Good heart, at what?

BENVOLIO   At thy good heart's oppression.

ROMEO Why, such is love's *(8)* transgression. –
Griefs of mine own lie heavy in my breast;
Which thou wilt *(9)* propagate, to have it prest   180
With more of thine: this love that thou hast shown
Doth add more grief to too much of mine own.
Love is a smoke rais'd with the fume of sighs;
Being *(10)* purg'd, a fire sparkling in lovers' eyes;
Being vex'd, a sea nourish'd with lovers' tears: 185
What is it else? a madness most *(11)* discreet,
(12) A choking gall, and a preserving sweet. –
Farewell, my coz.   *(Going.*

BENVOLIO   *(13)* Soft! I will go along:
An if you leave me so, you do me wrong.   190

ROMEO Tut, I have lost myself; I am not here;
This is not Romeo, he's some other where.

BENVOLIO Tell me in *(14)* sadness who is that you love.

ROMEO What, shall I *(15)* groan and tell thee?

BENVOLIO   Groan! why, no;   195
But *(16)* sadly tell me who.

ROMEO *(17)* Bid a sick man in sadness make his will, –
Ah, word ill urg'd to one that is so ill! –
In sadness, cousin, I do love a woman.

BENVOLIO *(18)* I aim'd so near when I suppos'd you lov'd.   200

ROMEO A right good marksman! – And she's fair I love.

BENVOLIO A right fair *(19)* mark, fair coz, is soonest hit.

ROMEO Well, *(20)* in that hit you miss: she'll not be hit
With Cupid's arrow, – she hath *(21)* Dian's wit;
And in strong proof of chastity well arm'd,   205
From *(22)* love's weak childish bow she lives unharm'd.
She will not *(23)* stay the siege of loving terms

1	Rosaline, the girl he thinks he is in love with, is a Capulet
2	there follows a series of ANTITHESES, the balance of opposites, which occur throughout the play and are a symbol of the conflict within it.
3	opposite of "nothing can come of nothing"
4	vanity = trivia
5	constantly waking
6	his love is one-sided, it is not returned
7	not necessarily a cousin, but certainly a relative
8	love's sin against me
9	make worse
10	cleared cf. Sonnet 37
11	discriminating
12	it is both bitter and sweet
13	wait
14	seriously
15	pun on "sadness" as in sorrow
16	continuation of the pun
17	he should make his will, as he is in such a bad way
18	a metaphor from ARCHERY, appropriate to cupid who fired a golden arrow
19	target
20	you are wrong
21	the evasive cunning of Diana, the Goddess of Chastity
22	i.e. Cupid
23	Rosaline will not be besieged by any of the stratagems of love. MILITARY metaphor

Nor bide the encounter of *(1)* assailing eyes,
Nor *(2)* ope her lap to saint-seducing gold:
O, she is rich in beauty; only poor,
That, when she dies, with beauty dies her *(3)* store.   **210**
BENVOLIO Then she hath sworn that she will still live chaste?
ROMEO She hath, and in that sparing makes huge *(4)* waste;
For beauty, *(5)* starv'd with her severity,
Cuts beauty off from all posterity.   **215**
She is too fair, too wise; wisely too *(6)* fair,
To merit *(7)* bliss by making me despair:
She hath forsworn to love; and in that vow
Do I live *(8)* dead that live to tell it now.
BENVOLIO Be rul'd by me, forget to think of her.   **220**
ROMEO O, teach me how I should forget to think.
BENVOLIO By giving liberty unto thine eyes;
Examine other *(9)* beauties.
ROMEO   *(10)* 'Tis the way
To call hers, exquisite, in *(11)* question more: **225**
These happy *(12)* masks that kiss fair ladies' brows,
Being black, put us in mind they hide the fair;
He that is strucken blind cannot forget
The precious treasure of his eyesight lost:
(13) Show me a mistress that is passing fair,   **230**
What doth her beauty serve but as a note
Where I may read who pass'd that passing fair?
Farewell: thou canst not teach me to forget.
BENVOLIO *(14)* I'll pay that doctrine or else die in debt.   *(Exeunt.*

ACT ONE, SCENE TWO

A STREET.

Enter CAPULET, PARIS, *and* Servant.

CAPULET *(15)* But Montague is bound as well as I,
In penalty alike; and *(16)* 'tis not hard, I think,
For men so old as we to keep the peace.
PARIS Of honourable *(17)* reckoning are you both;
And *(18)* pity 'tis you liv'd at odds so long.   **5**
But now, my lord, *(19)* what say you to my suit?
CAPULET But saying o'er what I have said before:
(20) My child is yet a stranger in the world,

1 the continuation of the MILITARY metaphor
2 she is not open to bribes of gifts
3 her store of beauty which will die with her if she has no children - cf. Sonnets 13-19
4 the waste is in not repeating her beauty in a child cf. Sonnet 1 particularly
5 killed
6 good
7 Heaven by remaining chaste - (despair would damn him)
8 I am only half-alive
9 beautiful girls (Benvolio is an expedient lover in advising Romeo to find someone else.)
10 IRONIC, as he will forget her immediately when he sees Juliet
11 IRONY - it will make me think of her even more
12 masks worn at balls (They were black, hiding the beauty underneath. To be fair-haired and pale was considered to be the height of beauty)
13 IRONICALLY he says that by comparing Rosaline with others he will only be further reminded of her beauty and that he is incapable of forgetting her.
14 I'll teach you how to forget or die in the attempt.
15 This is a reference to the Prince's rebuke
16 Both Capulet and Montague are old men. It is a further hint that the feud is on the wane.
17 reputation
18 cf the reference to "ancient grudge" in the Chorus' speech.
19 Paris loves Juliet and wishes to marry her.
20 Juliet has been kept secluded from the world

She hath not seen the [1] change of fourteen years;

[2] Let two more summers wither in their pride   10

Ere we may think her ripe to be a bride.

PARIS Younger than she are happy mothers made.

CAPULET And too soon [3] marr'd are those so early made.

[4] Earth hath swallow'd all my hopes but she, –

She is the hopeful lady of my [5] earth: 15

[6] But woo her, gentle Paris, get her heart,

My will to her consent is but a part;

An she agree, within her [7] scope of choice

Lies my consent and fair according voice.

This night I hold an old [8] accustom'd feast,   20

Whereto I have invited many a guest,

Such as I love; and you, among the [9] store,

One more, most welcome, makes my number more.

At my poor house look to behold this night

[10] Earth-treading stars that make dark heaven light: 25

Such [11] comfort as do lusty young men feel

When [12] well-apparell'd April on the heel

Of [13] limping winter treads, even such delight

Among fresh female buds shall you this night

[14] Inherit at my house; hear all, all see,   30

And [15] like her most whose merit most shall be:

Such, amongst view of many, [16] mine being one,

[17] May stand in number, though in reckoning none.

Come, go with me. – Go, sirrah, [18] trudge about

Through fair Verona; find those persons out   35

Whose names are written there *(gives a paper)*, and to them say,

My house and welcome on their pleasure [19] stay.

(Exeunt. CAPULET and PARIS.

SERVANT [20] Find them out whose names are written here! [21] It is

written that the shoemaker should meddle with his yard, and the

tailor with his last, the fisher with his pencil, and the painter   40

with his nets; but I am sent to find those persons whose names

are here writ, and can never find what names the writing person

hath here writ. I must to the learned: – [22] in good time.

Enter BENVOLIO *and* ROMEO.

BENVOLIO [23] Tut, man, one fire burns out another's burning,

One pain is lessen'd by another's [24] anguish;   45

Turn giddy, and be [25] holp by backward turning;

One desperate grief cures with another's [26] languish:

1	from winter to summer
2	IRONY - it becomes two days!
3	He is probably referring to the risk of death in childbirth to both mother and child.
4	He has buried all his children except for Juliet
5	He could mean his property, earthly possessions.
6	Paris must love her truly and make her love him. He is seen as a considerate father here and is going against custom by giving her a choice. It is IRONIC because once she disobeys him he becomes tyrannical
7	range
8	customary
9	number invited
10	women as beautiful as stars, dancing on earth and illuminating the darkness above
11	delight
12	clothed i.e. with leaves; a comparison with the SONNETS is available here
13	exhausted
14	receive i.e. delight to see them
15	choose the best, IRONY, cf. the advice of Benvolio to Romeo
16	i.e. Juliet
17	the general sense is that Juliet may be counted as one of the crowd
18	walk (this is to the servant)
19	wait
20	he cannot read
21	he muddles the connections between the trades and things which should go with them e.g. the shoemaker should have his last
22	here comes someone
23	Benvolio's love is unromantic. He suggests that one fire of love will put out another one. It is IRONIC because this is exactly what happens N.B. His words are in the form of a sestet for a sonnet
24	pain
25	helped by reversing
26	illness

Take thou some new [1] infection to thy eye,
And the rank poison of the old will die.
ROMEO Your [2] plantain-leaf is excellent for that.   50
BENVOLIO For what, I pray thee?
ROMEO   For your broken shin.
BENVOLIO Why, Romeo, art thou mad?
ROMEO Not mad, but [3] bound more than a madman is;
Shut up in prison, kept without my food,   55
Whipp'd and tormented, and – [4] God-den, good fellow
SERVANT God gi' god-den. – I pray, sir, can you read?
ROMEO Ay, mine own fortune in my misery.
SERVANT Perhaps you have learned it without book: but, I pray, can you
read anything you see?   60
ROMEO Ay, if I know the letters and the language.
SERVANT Ye say honestly: [5] rest you merry!
ROMEO Stay, fellow; I can read.   *(Reads.*
Signior Martino and his wife and daughters; County Anselme and
his beauteous sisters; the lady widow of Vitruvio; Signior Placentio   65
and his lovely nieces; Mercutio and his brother Valentine; mine
uncle Capulet, his wife and daughters; my fair niece Rosaline;
Livia; Signior Valentio and his cousin Tybalt; Lucio and the lively
Helena.
A fair assembly *(gives back the paper):* whither should they come?   70
SERVANT Up.
ROMEO Whither?
SERVANT To supper; to our house.
ROMEO Whose house?
SERVANT My master's.   75
ROMEO Indeed, I should have ask'd you that before.
SERVANT Now I'll tell you without asking: my master is the great rich
Capulet; and [6] if you be not of the house of Montagues, I pray,
come and [7] crush a cup of wine. Rest you merry!   *(Exit.*
BENVOLIO At this same [8] ancient feast of Capulet's   80
Sups the fair Rosaline whom thou so lov'st;
With all the admired beauties of Verona:
Go thither; and, with [9] unattainted eye,
Compare her face with some that I shall show,
And I will make thee think thy [10] swan a crow.   85
ROMEO [11] When the devout religion of mine eye
Maintains such falsehood, then turn tears to fires;
And [12] these, – who, often [13] drown'd, could never die, –
Transparent heretics, be burnt for liars!

---

1 love is seen as a disease, a poison in the body's system (He is trying to urge Romeo to take another love.)

2 a herbal remedy (Romeo is being IRONICAL, the remedy is for a physical ailment, it will not cure him.)

3 he feels as confined as a madman (The references refer to the treatment of the insane at that time.)

4 good evening (This CHANCE meeting alters Romeo's future.)

5 Goodbye - he thinks that Romeo is also illiterate

6 DRAMATIC IRONY - he does not realize that they are

7 drink

8 it was the custom for them to hold it

9 impartial

10 this comparison reinforces the LIGHT/DARK theme

11 Romeo uses the image of LOVE AS A RELIGION for the first time here and continues it with the reference to heretics

12 i.e. his eyes

13 i.e. with tears

One *(1)*fairer than my love! the all-seeing sun   **90**
Ne'er saw her match since first the world begun.
BENVOLIO Tut, you saw her fair, none else being by,
Herself *(2)* pois'd with herself in either eye:
But in that crystal scales let there be weigh'd
Your lady's love against some other maid   **95**
That I will show you shining at this feast,
And she shall *(3)* scant show well that now shows best.
ROMEO I'll go along, no such sight to be shown,
But to rejoice in splendour of *(4)* mine own.   *(Exeunt.*

ACT ONE, SCENE THREE
A ROOM IN CAPULET'S HOUSE.

Enter LADY CAPULET, *and* Nurse.

LADY CAPULET Nurse, where's my daughter? call her forth to me.
NURSE Now, *(5)* by my maidenhead, – at twelve year old, –
I *(6)* bade her come. – What lamb! what, *(7)* lady-bird! –
God forbid! – where's this girl? – what, Juliet!

Enter JULIET.
JULIET How now, who calls?   **5**
NURSE Your mother.
JULIET Madam, I am here. What is your will?
LADY CAPULET This is the matter, – Nurse, *(8)* give leave awhile,
We must talk in secret: – nurse, come back again;
I have *(9)* remember'd me, thou's hear our counsel.   **10**
Thou know'st my daughter's of a pretty age.
NURSE Faith, I can tell her age unto an hour.
LADY CAPULET She's not fourteen.
NURSE   I'll *(10)* lay fourteen of my teeth, –
And yet, to my teen be it spoken, I have but four,   **15**
She is not fourteen. How long is it now
To *(11)* Lammas-tide?
LADY CAPULET   A fortnight and odd days.
NURSE *(12)* Even or odd, of all days in the year,
Come Lammas-eve at night shall she be fourteen.   **20**
(13) Susan and she, – God rest all Christian souls! –
Were of an age: well, Susan is with God;
She was too good for me: – but, as I said,

---

1   DRAMATIC IRONY - he
    will immediately forget
    Rosaline
2   image of eyes as scales cf.
    Sonnet 29. for crystal
    eyes
3   hardly
4   i.e. Rosaline

5   she swears by the loss of
    her virginity. The nurse
    cannot resist bawdy
    references.
6   told her
7   endearments

8   leave us

9   on thinking about it you
    shall hear what is to be
    said

10 bet, wager

11 August 1st

12 whatever the number

13 her own child which
    died, so she became
    Juliet's wet nurse

17

On Lammas-eve at night shall she be fourteen;
That shall she, marry; I remember it well.   **25**
'Tis since the earthquake now eleven years;
And she was wean'd, – I never shall forget it, –
Of all the days of the year, upon that day:
For I had then laid (1) wormwood to my dug,
Sitting in the sun under the dove-house wall;   **30**
My lord and you were then at Mantua:
Nay, (2) I do bear a brain: – but, as I said,
When it did taste the wormwood on the nipple
Of my dug, and felt it bitter, pretty fool,
To see it (3) tetchy, and fall out with the dug!   **35**
(4) Shake, quoth the dovehouse: 'twas no need, I trow,
To bid me (5) trudge.
And since that time it is eleven years;
For then she could stand alone; nay, by the (6) rood
She could have run and waddled all about;   **40**
For even the day before, (7) she broke her brow:
And then my husband, – God be with his soul!
(8) 'A was a merry man, – took up the child:
Yea, quoth he, dost thou fall upon thy face?
Thou wilt (9) fall backward when thou hast more wit;   **45**
Wilt thou not, Jule? and, by my (10) holidame,
The pretty wretch left crying, and said (11) *Ay:*
(12) To see, now, how a jest shall come about!
I warrant, an I should live a thousand years,
I never should forget it: *Wilt thou not, Jule?* quoth he;   **50**
And, pretty fool, it stinted, and said *Ay.*
LADY CAPULET Enough of this; I pray thee, hold thy peace.
NURSE Yes, madam; – yet I cannot choose but laugh,
To think it should leave crying, and say Ay:
And yet, I warrant, it had upon its brow   **55**
A bump as big as a young cockerel's (13) stone;
A (14) parlous knock; and it cried bitterly.
Yea, quoth my husband, *fall'st upon thy face?*
Thou wilt fall backward when thou com'st to age;
Wilt thou not, Jule? it stinted, and said *Ay.*   **60**
JULIET And (15) stint thou too, I pray thee, nurse, say I.
NURSE Peace, I have done. God mark thee to his grace!
Thou wast the prettiest babe that e'er I nurs'd:
An I might live to see thee married once,
I have my wish.   **65**

1 a bitter substance applied to the nipple so that the child would reject it.

2 I remember

3 bad-tempered

4 a reference to the earthquake perhaps

5 go

6 cross (of Christ)

7 she grazed her forehead

8 He

9 a sexual innuendo N.B. the number of times she repeats the anecdote

10 holiness

11 yes

12 now she is going to be married (and will be lying on her back for Paris)

13 testicle

14 perilous, dangerous

15 Juliet, rather sharply, puts an end to this bawdiness.

LADY CAPULET (1) Marry, that marry is the very theme
    I came to talk of. – Tell me, daughter Juliet,
    (2) How stands your (3) disposition to be married?
JULIET It is an honour that I dream not of.
NURSE An honour! were not I thine only nurse,   **70**
    (4) I would say thou hadst suck'd wisdom from thy teat.
LADY CAPULET Well, think of marriage now; (5) younger than you,
    Here in Verona, ladies of esteem,
    Are made already mothers: by my count
    I was your mother much upon these years   **75**
    That you are now a maid. Thus, then, in brief; –
    The valiant Paris seeks you for his love.
NURSE A man, young lady! lady, such a man
    As all the world – why, he's a (6) man of wax.
LADY CAPULET Verona's summer hath not such a flower.   **80**
NURSE Nay, he's a flower; in faith, a very flower.
LADY CAPULET What say you? can you love the gentleman?
    (7) This night you shall behold him at our feast;
    Read o'er the (8) volume of young Paris' face,
    And find delight writ there with beauty's pen;   **85**
    Examine every (9) married lineament,
    And see how one another lends (10) content;
    And what obscur'd in this fair volume lies
    Find written in the (11) margent of his eyes.
    This precious book of love, this (12) unbound lover,   **90**
    To beautify him, only lacks a (13) cover:
    (14) The fish lives in the sea; and 'tis much pride
    For fair without the fair within to hide:
    That book in many's eyes doth share the glory
    That in gold (15) clasps locks in the golden story;   **95**
    So shall you share all that he doth possess,
    By having him, making yourself no less.
NURSE No less! nay, bigger; women (16) grow by men.
LADY CAPULET Speak briefly, can you like of Paris' love?
JULIET (17) I'll look to like, if looking liking move: **100**
    But no more deep will I (18) endart mine eye
    Than your consent gives strength to make it (19) fly.

    Enter a Servant.
SERVANT Madam, the guests are come, supper served up, you called, my
    young lady asked for, the nurse cursed in the pantry, and
    everything in (20) extremity. I must hence to wait; I beseech you,   **105**

---

1 PUN 1 by Mary 2 Marriage
2 the expedient marriage to Paris is proposed, expedient because he is wealthy and of high status
3 feelings
4 she is dubious about her own wisdom having been passed on to Juliet (through the milk)
5 Lady Capulet has not the fears of her husband regarding the dangers of childbirth. One suspects that she is dazzled by the high born Paris-as a son-in-law.
6 like a sculpture
7 DRAMATIC IRONY - she beholds Romeo, she does not look at Paris
8 i.e. as if he is a book (she now indulges in a sustained and elaborate metaphor)
9 his features combined together are perfect
10 PUN on the contents of the lovely book
11 margin
12 i.e. he is free to marry (she is continuing the metaphor of Paris as a book)
13 i.e. a wife
14 the general sense is that just as a fish is in its right element in the sea, so a book needs to be bound by a cover to be complete. You will give the book golden fastenings and enhance its existing perfection.
15 PUN - clasps 1 fastenings 2 embraces
16 pregnant - another bawdy reference
17 IRONY in that she is perfectly prepared to be obedient until she sees Romeo.
18 dart
19 Like an ARROW - a repeat of this metaphor
20 in extremes of panic

follow straight.

LADY CAPULET We follow thee.   *(Exit* Servant.

                                        Juliet, the county stays.

NURSE *(1)* Go, girl, seek happy nights to happy days.   *(Exeunt.*

ACT ONE, SCENE FOUR
A STREET.

Enter ROMEO, MERCUTIO, BENVOLIO
with five or six Maskers, Torch-bearers, *and others.*

ROMEO What, shall this *(2)* speech be spoke for our excuse?
    Or shall we on without apology?

BENVOLIO The date is *(3)* out of such prolixity:
    We'll have no Cupid *(4)* hoodwink'd with a scarf,
    Bearing a *(5)* Tartar's painted bow of lath,   5
    Scaring the ladies like *(6)* a crow-keeper;
    Nor no *(7)* without-book prologue, faintly spoke
    After the prompter, for our entrance:
    But, let them *(8)* measure us by what they will,
    We'll *(9)* measure them a measure, and be gone.   10

ROMEO Give me a torch, – I am not for this *(10)* ambling;
    (11) Being but heavy, I will bear the light.

MERCUTIO Nay, gentle Romeo, we must have you dance.

ROMEO Not I, believe me: you have dancing shoes,
    With nimble *(12)* soles: I have a soul of lead   15
    So *(13)* stakes me to the ground I cannot move.

MERCUTIO You are a lover; borrow Cupid's wings,
    And *(14)* soar with them above a common bound.

ROMEO I am too *(15)* sore enpierced with his shaft
    To soar with his light feathers; and so *(16)* bound,   20
    I cannot *(17)* bound a pitch above dull woe:
    Under love's heavy burden do I sink.

MERCUTIO And to *(19)* sink in it should you burden love;
    Too great oppression for a tender thing.

ROMEO I love a tender thing? it is too rough,   25
    Too rude, too boisterous; and it pricks like thorn.

MERCUTIO If love be rough with you, be rough with love;
    (20) Prick love for pricking, and you beat love down. –
    Give me a case to put my *(21)* visage in: *(Putting on a mask.*
    (22) A visard for a visard! – what care I   30

1	yet another reference to sex.
2	they have prepared a speech to introduce themselves
3	that custom is now old-fashioned
4	blind-folded
5	bent in the shape of cupid's bow
6	scarecrow
7	a speech learned by heart
8	PUN - judge us as they like
9	dance them a measure
10	dancing
11	heavy in his heart, he will be the torchbearer LIGHT/DARK theme
12	PUN 1 soles of shoes 2 spiritual soul
13	pins him down, as in bear-baiting
14	rise up
15	too much (PUN on SOAR above)
16	tied down
17	leap
18	DRAMATIC IRONY: he leaps up to Juliet's balcony soon enough!
19	Bawdy ("oppression" has the meaning of being pressed down)
20	bawdy pun
21	a mask to put his face in
22	a visor (mask) for a face that is ugly

What *(1)* curious eye doth quote deformities?
Here are *(2)* the beetle-brows shall blush for me.
BENVOLIO Come, knock and enter; and no sooner in
But every man betake him to his legs.
ROMEO A torch for me: let wantons, light of heart,   35
Tickle the senseless *(3)* rushes with their heels;
For I am *(4)* proverb'd with a grandsire phrase, –
I'll be a candle-holder, and look on, –
The game was ne'er so fair, and I am done.
MERCUTIO Tut, *(5)* dun's the mouse, the constable's own word: 40
If thou art *(6)* dun, we'll draw thee from the mire
Of this – save reverence – <u>love, wherein thou stick'st
Up to the ears.</u> – Come, we *(7)* burn daylight, ho.
ROMEO *(8)* Nay, that's not so.
MERCUTIO   I mean, sir, in delay   45
We waste our lights in vain, like lamps by day.
Take our *(9)* good meaning, for our judgment sits
Five times in that ere once in our five wits.
ROMEO And we mean well in going to this mask;
But 'tis no *(10)* wit to go.   50
MERCUTIO   Why, may one ask?
ROMEO I dreamt a dream *(11)* to-night.
MERCUTIO   And so did I.
ROMEO Well, what was yours?
MERCUTIO   That dreamers often lie.   55
ROMEO In bed asleep, while they do dream things true.
MERCUTIO O, then, I see *(12)* Queen Mab hath been with you.
She is the fairies' *(13)* midwife; and she comes
In shape no bigger than an *(14)* agate-stone,
On the fore-finger of an alderman,   60
Drawn with a team of little *(15)* atomies
(16) Athwart men's noses as they lie asleep: -
Her waggon-spokes made of long *(17)* spinners' legs;
The cover, of the wings of grasshoppers;
The *(18)* traces, of the smallest spider's web;   65
The collars, of the moonshine's *(19)* watery beams;
Her whip, of cricket's bone; the lash, of *(20)* film;
Her waggoner, a small gray-coated gnat,
Not half so big as a *(21)* round little worm
Prick'd from the lazy finger of a maid: 70
Her chariot is an empty hazel-nut,
Made by the *(22)* joiner squirrel or old grub,

1	inquisitive
2	his mask has huge eyebrows
3	i.e. the floor covering
4	proverb: the onlooker sees most of the game (in gambling)
5	a proverbial expression meaning "Keep quiet"
6	dark (PUN - it refers to a game where an imaginary horse in the shape of a log, was pulled out of a ditch.)
7	waste time
8	It is, in fact, dark
9	the general meaning could be "accept our good intentions rather than what we literally say."
10	not intelligent - PUN on wit above.
11	last night
12	possibly an invented fairy
13	she brings forth dreams
14	a stone used in a seal-ring
15	tiny creatures
16	over
17	spiders
18	harness, probably reins
19	i.e. from the dew
20	gossamer
21	from a saying that girls' idle fingers breed maggots
22	the squirrel shapes it with his teeth, whilst the grub bores holes

Time out o' mind the fairies' coachmakers.
And in this state she gallops night by night
Through lovers' brains, and then they dream of love;   **75**
O'er courtiers' knees, that dream on (1) court'sies straight;
O'er lawyers' fingers, who straight dream on fees;
O'er ladies' lips, who straight on kisses dream, –
Which oft the angry Mab with blisters plagues,
Because their breaths with (2) sweatmeats tainted are: **80**
Sometime she gallops o'er a courtier's nose,
And then dreams he of smelling out a (3) suit;
And sometime comes she with a (4) tithe-pig's tail,
Tickling a parson's nose as 'a lies asleep,
Then dreams he of another (5) benefice: **85**
Sometime she driveth o'er a soldier's neck,
And then dreams he of cutting foreign throats,
Of breaches, (6) ambuscadoes, (7) Spanish blades,
Of (8) healths five fathom deep; and then anon
Drums in his ear, at which he starts and wakes;   **90**
And, being thus frighted, swears a prayer or two,
And sleeps again. This is that very Mab
That (9) plats the manes of horses in the night;
And bakes the (10) elf-locks in foul sluttish hairs,
Which, once untangled, much (11) misfortune bodes: **95**
This is the hag, when maids lie on their backs,
That presses them, and learns them first to (12) bear,
Making them women of good (13) carriage:
This is she, –
ROMEO   Peace, peace, Mercutio, peace,   **100**
Thou talk'st of nothing.
MERCUTIO   True, I talk of dreams,
Which are the children of an idle brain,
Begot of nothing but (14) vain fantasy;
Which is as thin of substance as the air,   **105**
And more inconstant than the wind, who woos
Even now the frozen bosom of the (15) north,
And, being anger'd, puffs away from thence,
Turning his face to the dew-dropping south.
BENVOLIO This wind you talk of (16) blows us from ourselves: **110**
Supper is done, and we shall come too late.
ROMEO I fear, too early: for my mind misgives
Some consequence, yet hanging in the stars,
Shall bitterly begin his fearful (18) date

1	curtseys (presumably dreaming of gaining favour) N.B. PUN 1. courtier 2. curtsey
2	lozenges for freshening breath
3	someone who will pay him for taking a request to the Monarch
4	Church taxes were often paid with produce.
5	living, an extra parish, therefore more money
6	ambushes
7	Toledo steel swords
8	drinks
9	plaits, tangles (a superstition that fairies caused mischief of this kind)
10	matted tangles in dirty hair
11	bad luck
12	bawdy reference
13	PUN 1. deportment 2. childbearing
14	fruitless
15	ANTITHESIS: North followed almost immediately by South
16	turns us away from our intention to visit the Capulets
17	Romeo has a PREMONITION of what might be in store "in the stars"
18	time

With this night's revels; and *(1)* expire the term   **115**
Of a despised life, clos'd in my breast,
By some vile forfeit of untimely death:
But He that hath the *(2)* steerage of my course
(3) Direct my sail! – On, *(4)* lusty gentlemen.
BENVOLIO Strike, drum.   *(Exeunt.*   **120**

ACT ONE, SCENE FIVE

A HALL IN CAPULET'S HOUSE

Musicians waiting. Enter Servants.

1 SERVANT Where's Potpan, that he helps not to *(5)* take away? he shift
a trencher! he scrape a *(6)* trencher!
2 SERVANT When good manners shall lie all in one or two men's hands,
and they unwashed too, 'tis a foul thing.
1 SERVANT Away with the *(7)* joint-stools, remove the *(8)* court-cupboard,   **5**
look to the *(9)* plate: – good thou, save me a piece of
(10) marchpane; and as thou lovest me let the porter let in
(11) Susan Grindstone and Nell. – Antony! and Potpan!
2 SERVANT Ay, boy, ready.
1 SERVANT You are looked for and called for, asked for and sought for   **10**
in the great chamber.
2 SERVANT We cannot be here and there too. – Cheerly, boys; be brisk
awhile, and *(12)* the longer liver take all.   *(They retire behind.*

Enter CAPULET, *& c., with the* Guests *and the* Maskers.
CAPULET Welcome, gentlemen! ladies that have their toes
Unplagu'd with corns will have *(13)* a bout with you. –   **15**
Ah ha, my mistresses! which of you all
Will now deny to dance? she that *(14)* makes dainty, she,
I'll swear hath corns; am *(15)* I come near you now?
Welcome, gentlemen! *(16)* I have seen the day
That I have worn a *(17)* visard; and could tell   **20**
A whispering tale in a fair lady's ear,
Such as would please; – *(18)* 'tis gone, 'tis gone, 'tis gone:
You are welcome, gentlemen – Come, musicians, play. –
A hall, – a hall! *(19)* give room, and foot it, girls. –
                    (Music plays, and they dance.
More light, you knaves; and *(20)* turn the tables up,   **25**
And quench the fire, the room is grown too hot. –

1   legal metaphor - the mortgage is his life and he will have to forfeit it
2   guidance
3   he trusts to fortune (This is linked with the image of Romeo as a pilot which recurs throughout the play)
4   lively
5   clear (the table)
6   wooden dish from which food was served
7   wooden stools jointed, not nailed, together
8   side board
9   silver dishes
10   marzipan
11   to the servants' party about to begin
12   proverb meaning, "we will all die in the end so what is the rush?"
13   a dance
14   hesitates and makes excuses
15   have I got it right?
16   he refers to his youth when he was a man for the ladies
17   visor, mask
18   i.e. his youth
19   make room for dancing
20   the trestle tables are to be packed up to make space for dancing

Ah, sirrah, this [1] unlook'd-for sport comes well.

[2] Nay, sit, nay, sit, good cousin Capulet;

For you and I are past our dancing days:

How long is't now since last yourself and I   **30**

Were in a mask?

2 CAPULET By'r Lady, thirty years.

CAPULET What, man! 'tis not so much, 'tis not so much:

'Tis since the [3] nuptial of Lucentio,

Come Pentecost as quickly as it will,   **35**

Some five-and-twenty years; and then we mask'd.

2 CAPULET 'Tis more, 'tis more: his son is elder, sir;

His son is thirty.

CAPULET   Will you tell me that?

His son was but a [4] ward two years ago.   **40**

ROMEO What lady is that which doth enrich the hand

Of yonder knight?

SERVANT   [5] I know not, sir.

ROMEO O, she doth teach the torches to burn bright!

It seems she hangs upon the cheek of night   **45**

Like a rich jewel in an [6] Ethiop's ear;

[7] Beauty too rich for use, for earth too dear!

[8] So shows a snowy dove trooping with crows

As yonder lady o'er her fellows shows.

[9] The measure done, I'll watch her place of stand,   **50**

And, touching hers, make blessed my rude hand.

Did my heart love till now? [10] forswear it, sight!

For I ne'er saw true beauty till this night.

TYBALT This, by his voice, should be a Montague. –

Fetch me my rapier, boy: – what, dares the slave   **55**

Come hither, cover'd with an [11] antic face,

To [12] fleer and scorn at our [13] solemnity?

Now, by the [14] stock and honour of my kin,

To strike him dead I hold it not a sin.

CAPULET Why, how now, kinsman! wherefore storm you so?   **60**

TYBALT Uncle, this is a Montague, our foe;

A villain, that is hither come in spite,

To scorn at our solemnity this night.

CAPULET Young Romeo, is it?

TYBALT   'Tis he, that villain, Romeo.   **65**

CAPULET [15] Content thee, gentle coz, let him alone,

He bears him like a [16] portly gentleman;

And, to say truth, Verona brags of him

---

1   the arrival of the maskers

2   these anecdotes confirm Capulets' advanced age

3   marriage

4   i.e. under twenty-one

5   (perhaps he is a servant hired for the night, that the daughter of the house is unknown to him)

6   a black African - the contrast of LIGHT/DARK is used again

7   Juliet is too beautiful for this earth and "earth has swallowed all my hopes but she" DRAMATIC IRONY

8   cf. "swan and crow" Act 1, Scene 2 line 85

9   When the dance is over I'll watch where she stands

10   deny (Irony - he has forgotten Rosaline)

11   fantastic mask

12   laugh, jeer

13   solemn feast

14   parentage

15   be calm

16   dignified

To be a virtuous and *(1)* well-govern'd youth:
I would not for the wealth of all the town　　　　　　70
Here in my house do him *(2)* disparagement:
Therefore be patient, take no note of him. –
It is my will; the which if thou respect,
Show a *(3)* fair presence and *(4)* put off these frowns,
An ill-beseeming semblance for a feast.　　　　　　75

TYBALT It fits, when such a villain is a guest:
I'll not endure him.

CAPULET　　　　　　He shall be endur'd.
What, *(5)* goodman, boy! – I say he shall; – go to;
Am I the master here or you? go to.　　　　　　80
You'll not endure him! – God shall mend my soul,
You'll make a mutiny among my guests!
You will set cock-a-hoop! you'll be *(6)* the man!

TYBALT Why, uncle, 'tis a shame.

CAPULET　　　　　　Go to, go to;　　　　　85
You are a *(7)* saucy boy. Is't so, indeed? –
This *(8)* trick may chance to scathe you, – I know what:
You must *(9)* contrary me! marry, *(10)* 'tis time. –
Well said, my hearts! – You are a *(11)* princox; go:
Be quiet, or – More light, more light! – For shame!　　90
I'll make you quiet. – What, – cheerly, my hearts.

TYBALT Patience perforce with wilful *(12)* choler meeting
Makes my *(13)* flesh tremble in their different greeting.
I will withdraw: but this intrusion shall,
Now seeming sweet, convert to bitter *(14)* gall.　　*(Exit.*　95

ROMEO *(15)* If I profane with my unworthiest hand　　*(To* JULIET.
This holy shrine, the gentle fine is this, –
My lips, two blushing pilgrims, ready stand
To smooth that rough touch with a tender kiss.

JULIET *(16)* Good pilgrim, you do wrong your hand too much,　　100
Which *(17)* mannerly devotion shows in this;
For saints have hands that pilgrims' hands do touch,
And palm to palm is holy *(18)* palmers' kiss.

ROMEO Have not saints lips, and holy palmers too?

JULIET Ay, pilgrim, lips that *(19)* they must use in prayer.　　105

ROMEO O, then, dear saint, *(20)* let lips do what hands do;
They pray, grant thou, lest faith turn to despair.

JULIET Saints do not move, though grant for prayers' sake.

ROMEO Then *(21)* move not while my prayer's effect I take.
(22) Thus from my lips, by yours, my sin is purg'd.　　*(Kissing her.*　110

1　well-mannered
2　indignity
3　i.e. be well-mannered yourself
4　frowns are unsuitable at a feast
5　Capulet insults Tybalt by suggesting that he is not a gentleman and that he is too young to know what is right to do
6　play "the big man!"
7　insolent
8　this manner of yours will harm you in the end IRONIC because it brings about his death
9　oppose
10　this is to the dancers
11　impertinent young boy
12　anger i.e. Capulets'
13　the clash between anger (Tybalt) and patience (Capulet) makes him shake
14　bitterness DRAMATIC IRONY
15　N.B. SONNET form - Romeo offers the comparison of himself as a pilgrim to her hand, the "holy shrine"
16　Juliet continues the comparison, they are like statues of saints at a shrine
17　proper
18　another word for pilgrim (who carry palms - PUN)
19　not use in kissing
20　he agrees that lips and hands should pray, but he really wants a kiss
21　keep still (whilst I kiss you)
22　the general meaning is that her kiss has purged his sin which she says is now passed on to her.

JULIET Then have my lips the sin that they have took.
ROMEO Sin from my lips? O trespass sweetly urg'd!
Give me my sin again.
JULIET   You kiss by *(1)* the book.
NURSE Madam, your mother craves a word with you.   115
ROMEO What is her mother?
NURSE   Marry, *(2)* bachelor,
Her mother is the lady of the house,
And a good lady, and a wise and virtuous:
I nurs'd her daughter that you talk'd withal;   120
I tell you, he that can lay hold of her
Shall have the *(3)* chinks.
ROMEO   Is she a Capulet?
(4) O dear account! my life is my foe's debt.
BENVOLIO Away, be gone; the sport is at the best.   125
ROMEO Ay, *(5)* so I fear; the more is my unrest.
CAPULET Nay, gentlemen, prepare not to be gone;
We have a trifling foolish *(6)* banquet towards. –
Is it e'en so? *(7)* why, then I thank you all;
I thank you, honest gentlemen; good-night. –   130
More torches here! – Come on, then let's to bed.
Ah, sirrah *(to 2 Cap.),* *(8)* by my fay, it waxes late:
I'll to my rest.   *(Exeunt all but* JULIET *and* Nurse.
JULIET Come hither, nurse. What is yon gentleman?
NURSE The son and heir of old Tiberio.   135
JULIET *(9)* What's he that now is going out of door?
NURSE Marry, that I think be young Petruchio.
JULIET What's he that follows there, that would not dance?
NURSE I know not.
JULIET Go ask his name: if he be married,   140
(10) My grave is like to be my wedding-bed.
NURSE His name is Romeo, and a Montague;
The only son of your great enemy.
JULIET My only *(11)* love sprung from my only hate!
(12) Too early seen unknown, and known too late!   145
(13) Prodigious birth of love it is to me,
That I must love a loathed enemy.
NURSE. What's this? What's this?
JULIET   A rhyme I learn'd even now
Of *(14)* one I danc'd withal.   *(One calls within,* "JULIET."   150
NURSE   Anon, anon!
Come, let's away; the strangers are all gone.   *(Exeunt.*

1 properly

2 young man

3 money - because Juliet is
    an heiress

4 I am bound for life to the
    enemy

5 i.e. that the best is over -
    he feels a PREMONITION
    again

6 light refreshments ready

7 he accepts their
    whispered excuse

8 By my faith, it grows late

9 Juliet is trying to divert
    attention from her
    interest in Romeo

10 She has a PREMONITION
    - there is DRAMATIC
    IRONY here, and it is the
    introduction to the
    theme of DEATH AS
    JULIET'S LOVER

11 ANTITHESIS, the use of
    opposites again.

12 I fell in love with him as
    an unknown, now that I
    know who he is it is too
    late.

13 a bad omen

14 She is being evasive; as a
    "stranger to the world"
    she well knows how to
    divert attention from her
    lover!

ACT TWO, SCENE ONE

AN OPEN PLACE ADJOINING CAPULET'S GARDEN.

Enter Chorus.

Now [1] old desire doth in his death-bed lie,
And young [2] affection [3] gapes to be his heir;
That [4] fair for which love groan'd for, and would die,
With tender Juliet [5] match'd, is now not fair.
Now Romeo is belov'd, and loves again,   5
[6] Alike bewitched by the charm of looks;
But to his foe [7] suppos'd he must complain,
And [8] she steal love's sweet bait from fearful hooks:
Being held a foe, he may not have access
To breathe such vows as lovers [9] us'd to swear;   10
And she as much in love, her means much less
To meet her new-beloved anywhere:
But passion lends them power, time [10] means to meet,
[11] Tempering extremities with extreme sweet.   *(Exit.*

Enter ROMEO.

ROMEO Can I [12] go forward when my heart is here?   15
  [13] Turn back, dull earth, and find thy centre out.
                    (He climbs the wall and leaps down within it.

Enter BENVOLIO and MERCUTIO.

BENVOLIO Romeo! my cousin Romeo!
MERCUTIO   He is wise;
  And, on my life, hath stol'n him home to bed.
BENVOLIO He ran this way, and leap'd this [14] orchard wall: 20
  Call, good Mercutio
MERCUTIO   Nay, I'll [15] conjure too. –
  Romeo! [16] humours! madman! passion! lover!
  [17] Appear thou in the likeness of a sigh:
  Speak but one rhyme and I am satisfied;   25
  Cry but, Ah me! pronounce but [17] love and dove;
  Speak to my [18] gossip Venus one fair word,
  One nickname for her [19] purblind son and heir,
  Young auburn Cupid, he that shot so trim
  When King [20] Cophetua lov'd the beggar-maid! –   30
  He heareth not, he stirreth not, he moveth not;
  [21] The ape is dead, and I must conjure him. –
  [22] I conjure thee by Rosaline's bright eyes,

By her high forehead and her scarlet lip,	*1* the areas adjacent to her
By her fine foot, straight leg, and quivering thigh,　35	thigh
And the *(1)* demesnes that there adjacent lie,	*2* by magic, to make a
That in thy likeness thou appear to us!	spirit appear to make love
BENVOLIO An if he hear thee, thou wilt anger him.	to Rosaline
MERCUTIO This cannot anger him: 'twould anger him	*3* another bawdy reference
To *(2)* raise a spirit in his mistress' circle,　40	*4* injury
Of some strange nature, letting it there stand	*5* summoning
(3) Till she had laid it, and conjur'd it down;	*6* make him appear to us
That were some *(4)* spite: my *(5)* invocation	(bawdy innuendo)
Is fair and honest, and, in his mistress' name,	*7* medlar was often used as
(6) I conjure only but to raise up him.　45	a name for female
BENVOLIO Come, he hath hid himself among these trees.	genitalia, its other name
To be consorted with the humorous night:	was "open arse"
Blind is his love, and best befits the dark.	*8* i.e. the medlar - the
MERCUTIO If love be blind, love cannot hit the mark.	dialect form was
Now will he sit under a *(7)* medlar tree,　50	"poperin", open to all
And wish his mistress were that *(8)* kind of fruit	sorts of innuendo
As maids call medlars when they laugh alone. –	*9* small bed
Romeo, good-night. – I'll to my *(9)* truckle-bed;	*10* camp bed
This *(10)* field-bed is too cold for me to sleep:	
Come shall we go?　55	
BENVOLIO　　　　　Go, then; for 'tis in vain	*11* i.e. Mercutio makes fun
To seek him here that means not to be found.　*(Exeunt.*	because, never having
	loved, he cannot
	sympathise

ACT TWO, SCENE TWO

CAPULET'S GARDEN.

Enter ROMEO.

	12 the contrast between
	LIGHT/DARK is very
	marked in Romeo's
	lyrical address to Juliet.
ROMEO *(11)* He jests at scars that never felt a wound. –	N.B. the immediate
*(*JULIET *appears above at a window.*	change of tone from
But soft! *(12)* what light through yonder window breaks?	Mercutio's bawdiness -
It is the east, and Juliet is the sun! –	another CONTRAST.
Arise, fair sun, and kill the *(13)* envious moon,	*13* Diana, the Moon
Who is already sick and pale with grief,　5	Goddess, was also the
That thou her maid art far more fair than she:	Goddess of chastity
(14) Be not her maid, since she is envious;	*14* do not follow Diana
Her *(15)* vestal livery is but sick and green,	*15* virgin clothing is pallid
And none but *(16)* fools do wear it; cast it off. –	as moonlight
It is my lady; O, it is my love!　10	*16* like a court jester

O, that she knew she (1) were! –	
She speaks, yet she says nothing: what of that?	
Her eye discourses, I will answer it. –	
I am too bold, 'tis not to me she speaks:	
Two of the fairest (2) stars in all the heaven,	15
(3) Having some business do entreat her eyes	
To twinkle in their spheres till they return.	
What if her eyes were there, (4) they in her head?	
The brightness of her cheek would shame those stars,	
As daylight doth a lamp; her eyes in heaven	20
Would through the (5) airy region stream so bright	
That birds would sing, and think it were not night. –	
See how she leans her cheek upon her hand!	
O, that I were a glove upon that hand,	
That I might touch that cheek!	25

JULIET   (6) Ah me!

ROMEO   She speaks: –

> O, speak again, (7) bright angel! for thou art
> As glorious to this night, being o'er my head,
> As is a (8) winged messenger of heaven   30
> Unto the white-upturned wondering eyes
> Of mortals that fall back to gaze on him
> When he bestrides the (9) lazy-pacing clouds
> And sails upon the bosom of the air.

JULIET O Romeo, Romeo! (10) wherefore art thou Romeo?   35
> Deny thy father and refuse thy name;
> Or, if thou wilt not, be but sworn my love,
> And I'll no longer be a Capulet.

ROMEO *(Aside.)* Shall I hear more, or shall I speak at this?

JULIET 'Tis but thy name that is my enemy; –   40
> Thou art thyself, (11) though not a Montague.
> What's Montague? It is nor hand, nor foot,
> Nor arm, nor face, nor any other part
> Belonging to a man. O, be some other name!
> What's in a name? that which we call a rose,   45
> By any other name would smell as sweet;
> So Romeo would, were he not Romeo call'd
> Retain the dear perfection which he (12) owes
> Without that title: – Romeo, (13) doff thy name;
> (14) And for that name, which is no part of thee,   50
> Take all myself.

ROMEO   I take thee at thy word:

Notes

1 i.e. my love

2 planets

3 having been taken away from their usual spheres

4 i.e. the stars

5 sky

6 IRONY - she sighs exactly as Mercutio has just mocked Romeo for so doing

7 LOVE AS RELIGION appears again

8 angel

9 puffy clouds moving slowly

10 Why - the themes of LOVE and ENMITY are combined here

11 even if you were not

12 owns

13 take it off, like a hat

14 in exchange for your name

Call me but love, and I'll be new baptiz'd;
Henceforth I never will be Romeo.

JULIET What man art thou, that, thus *(1)* bescreen'd in night,   55

So stumblest on my *(2)* counsel?

ROMEO   By a name

I know not how to tell thee who I am:

My name, dear saint, is hateful to myself.

Because it is an enemy to thee;   60

Had I it written, I would tear the word.

JULIET My ears have not yet drunk a hundred words

Of that tongue's utterance, yet I know the sound;

Art thou not Romeo, and a Montague?

ROMEO Neither, *(3)* fair saint, if either thee *(4)* dislike.   65

JULIET How cam'st thou hither, tell me, and wherefore?

The orchard walls are high and hard to climb;

And the *(5)* place death, considering who thou art,

If any of my kinsmen find thee here.

ROMEO With love's light wings did I *(6)* o'erperch these walls;   70

For stony limits cannot hold love out:

And what love can do, that *(7)* dares love attempt;

Therefore thy kinsmen are no *(8)* let to me.

JULIET If they do see thee they will murder thee.

ROMEO Alack, there lies more *(9)* peril in thine eye   75

Than twenty of their swords: look thou but sweet,

And I am *(10)* proof against their enmity.

JULIET I would not for the world they saw thee here.

ROMEO I have night's cloak to hide me from their sight;

And, but thou love me, let them find me here: 80

My life were better ended by their hate

Than death *(11)* prorogued wanting of thy love.

JULIET By whose direction found'st thou out this place?

ROMEO By love, who first did prompt me to inquire;

He lent me *(12)* counsel, and I lent him eyes.   85

I am no *(13)* pilot; yet, wert thou as far

As that vast shore wash'd with the *(14)* furthest sea,

I would adventure for such *(15)* merchandise.

JULIET Thou know'st the mask of night is on my face,

Else would a maiden blush bepaint my cheek   90

For that which thou hast heard me speak to-night.

(16) Fain would I dwell on *(17)* form, fain, fain deny

What I have spoke: but farewell *(18)* compliment!

Dost thou love me? I know thou wilt say Ay;

1	hidden
2	secret thoughts
3	by repeating this he could be reminding her of their previous meeting and previous conversation in Act One Scene 5 "Have not saint's lips?"
4	if it displeases you
5	you will be killed if you are discovered
6	fly over
7	loves dares to
8	impediment
9	danger to him (if she refuses him)
10	protected
11	deferred, I should rather be dead if I lacked your love
12	advice
13	an accomplished steersman; Romeo uses the image of himself as a PILOT negotiating dangerous waters several times in the play.
14	i.e. the world's end
15	the metaphor is that pilots would steer merchant ships, full of wealth, into harbour. Juliet is the wealth.
16	gladly
17	proper behaviour
18	etiquette

And I will take thy word: yet, if thou swear'st,   95
Thou mayst prove false; at lovers' *(1)* perjuries   *1* lies
They say *(2)* Jove laughs. O gentle Romeo,   *2* proverbial saying
If thou dost love, pronounce it *(3)* faithfully: *3* truly
Or, if thou think'st I am too quickly won,   *4* so that you will continue
I'll frown, and be perverse, and say thee nay,   100   to woo me
(4) So thou wilt woo; but else, not for the world.   *5* foolish
In truth, fair Montague, I am too *(5)* fond;   *6* behaviour is immodest
And therefore thou mayst think my *(6)* 'haviour light:
But trust me, gentleman, I'll prove more true
Than those that have more *(7)* cunning to be strange.   105   *7* practice in love's games
I should have been more *(8)* strange, I must confess,   and play "hard to get"
But that thou over-heard'st, ere I was 'ware,   *8* distant
My true love's passion: therefore pardon me;
And not impute this yielding to light love,
Which the dark night hath so *(9)* discovered.   110   *9* revealed

Romeo Lady, by yonder blessed moon I swear,
That tips with silver all these fruit-tree tops, –
Juliet O, swear not by the moon, the inconstant moon,
That monthly changes in her *(10)* circled orb,   *10* the orbit in which the
Lest that thy love prove likewise variable.   115   moon moves
Romeo What shall I swear by?
Juliet   Do not swear at all;
Or, if thou wilt, swear by thy gracious self,
Which is the *(11)* god of my idolatry,   *11* she adores him
And I'll believe thee.   120
Romeo   If my heart's dear love, –
Juliet Well, do not swear: although I joy in thee,
(12) I have no joy of this contract to-night: *12* Juliet has a
It is too rash, too unadvis'd, too sudden;   PREMONITION that
(13) Too like the lightning, which doth cease to be   125   disaster will follow
Ere one can say, "It lightens". Sweet, good-night!   *13* the first of several images
This bud of love, by summer's ripening breath,   of LIGHTNING
May prove a beauteous flower when next we meet.
Good-night, good-night! as sweet repose and rest
Come to thy heart as that within my breast!   130
Romeo O, wilt thou leave me so unsatisfied?
Juliet What satisfaction canst thou have to-night?
Romeo The exchange of thy love's faithful vow for mine.
Juliet I gave thee mine before thou didst request it:
And yet I would it were to give again.   135
Romeo Wouldst thou withdraw it? for what purpose, love?

JULIET But to be [1] frank, and give it thee again.
    And yet I wish but for the thing I have:
    My [2] bounty is as boundless as the sea,
    My love as deep; and more I give to thee   **140**
    The more I have, for both are [3] infinite.   *(Nurse call within.*
    I hear some noise within; dear love, adieu! –
    [4] Anon, good nurse! – Sweet Montague, be true.
    Stay but a little, I will come again.   *(Exit.*
ROMEO O blessed, blessed night! I am afeard,   **145**
    Being in night, all this is but a dream,
    Too flattering-sweet to be substantial.

    Re-enter JULIET *above.*
JULIET Three words, dear Romeo, and good-night indeed.
    If that thy [5] bent of love be honourable,
    Thy purpose marriage, send me word to-morrow,   **150**
    By one that I'll [6] procure to come to thee,
    Where and what time thou wilt perform the rite;
    And all my fortunes at thy foot I'll lay,
    And follow thee, my lord, throughout the world.
NURSE *(Within.)* Madam!   **155**
JULIET I come [7] anon. – But if thou mean'st not well,
    I do beseech thee, –
NURSE *(Within.)*   Madam!
JULIET   By and by, I come: –
    To cease thy suit, and leave me to my grief: **160**
    To-morrow will I send.
ROMEO   So thrive my soul, –
JULIET A thousand times good-night!   *(Exit.*
ROMEO A thousand times the worse, to want thy light. –
    Love goes toward love as school-boys from their books; **165**
    But love from love, toward school with heavy looks.
                   (Retiring slowly.

    Re-enter JULIET *above.*
JULIET Hist! Romeo, hist! – O for a [8] falconer's voice,
    To lure this [9] tassel-gentle back again!
    [10] Bondage is hoarse, and may not speak aloud;
    Else would I tear the cave where Echo lies,   **170**
    And make her [11] airy tongue more hoarse than mine
    With repetition of my Romeo's name.
ROMEO It is my soul that calls upon my name:

1	generous
2	generosity
3	endless
4	in a minute
5	intention
6	arrange
7	immediately
8	possibly a whistle
9	male falcon
10	she is not free, she is under close chaperone
11	i.e. the echo of Viola in "Twelfth Night"

How silver-sweet sound lovers' tongues by night,
Like softest music to attending ears!   175

JULIET Romeo!

ROMEO   My dear?

JULIET   At what o'clock to-morrow
Shall I send to thee?

ROMEO   At the hour of nine.   180

JULIET I will not fail: 'tis twenty years till then.
I have forgot why I did call thee back.

ROMEO Let me stand here till thou remember it.

JULIET I shall forget, to have thee still stand there,
_(1)_ Remembering how I love thy company.   185   *1 thinking about*

ROMEO And I'll still stay, to have thee still forget,
Forgetting any other home but this.

JULIET 'Tis almost morning; I would have thee gone:
And yet no further than a _(2)_ wanton's bird;   *2 a mischievous child*
Who lets it hop a little from her hand,   190
Like a poor prisoner in his twisted _(3)_ gyves,   *3 shackles*
And with a silk thread plucks it back again,
So _(4)_ loving-jealous of his liberty.   *4 anxious that it will fly
                                                                        away*

ROMEO I would I were thy bird.

JULIET   Sweet, so would I: 200
Yet I should kill thee with much cherishing.
Good-night, good-night! parting is such sweet sorrow
That I shall say good-night till it be morrow.   *(Exit.*

ROMEO Sleep dwell upon thine eyes, peace in thy breast! –
Would I were sleep and peace, so sweet to rest!   205
Hence will I to my _(5)_ ghostly father's cell,   *5 holy*
His help to crave and my _(6)_ dear hap to tell.   *(Exit.*   *6 good fortune*

ACT TWO, SCENE THREE
FRIAR LAWRENCE'S CELL.

Enter FRIAR LAWRENCE *with a basket.*

FRIAR LAWRENCE The gray-ey'd morn smiles on the frowning night,
Chequering the eastern clouds with streaks of light;
And _(7)_ flecked darkness like a drunkard reels   *7 blotchy*
From forth day's path and _(8)_ Titan's fiery wheels: *8 the Sun God's chariot*

<u>Now, ere the sun</u> *(1)* <u>advance his burning eye,</u>　　　　　5
<u>The day to cheer and night's dank dew to dry,</u>
I must up-fill this *(2)* osier cage of ours
With *(3)* baleful weeds and precious-juiced flowers.
(4) The earth, that's nature's mother, is her tomb,
What is her burying grave, that is her womb:　　　　　10
And from her womb *(5)* children of divers kind
We sucking on her natural bosom find;
Many for many virtues excellent,
(6) None but for some, and yet all different.
O, *(7)* mickle is the powerful *(8)* grace that lies　　　　15
In herbs, plants, *(9)* stones, and their true qualities:
For *(10)* naught so vile that on the earth doth live
But to the earth some special good doth give;
Nor aught so good but, *(11)* strain'd from that fair use,
(12) Revolts from true birth, stumbling on abuse:　　　　20
Virtue itself turns vice, being misapplied;
And *(13)* vice sometimes by action dignified.
Within the *(14)* infant rind of this small flower
Poison hath residence, and medicine power:
For this, being smelt, with *(15)* that part cheers each part;　　25
Being tasted, *(16)* slays all senses with the heart.
Two such opposed kings encamp them still
In man as well as herbs, – *(17)* grace and rude will;
And where the worser is predominant,
Full soon the *(18)* canker death eats up that plant.　　　　30

Enter ROMEO
ROMEO Good-morrow, father!
FRIAR LAWRENCE　　　　　*(19) Benedicite!*
What early tongue so sweet saluteth me? –
Young son, it *(20)* argues a distemper'd head
So soon to bid good-morrow to thy bed:　　　　　35
Care keeps his *(21)* watch in every old man's eye,
And where care lodges sleep will never lie;
But where *(22)* unbruised youth with unstuff'd brain
Doth couch his limbs, there golden sleep doth reign:
Therefore thy earliness doth me assure　　　　　40
Thou art uprous'd by some *(23)* distemperature;
Or if not so, then here I hit it right, –
Our Romeo hath not been in bed to-night.
ROMEO That last is true; the sweeter rest was mine.

1	raise
2	willow basket
3	poisonous
4	nature is a cycle of birth, death
5	plants of many kinds
6	there are no plants which are of no use at all
7	great
8	power
9	minerals
10	nothing
11	prevented from its proper, normal use
12	if it happens to be abused it will lose its proper power
13	bad can be transformed sometimes by good (by using these examples of opposites we have ANTITHESIS)
14	the outside, which is hardly formed it is so young
15	the nose picks up the smell and revives the whole body
16	the heart, and all other senses, stop dead
17	the capacity for God's blessing and the capacity for sensuality
18	worm
19	bless you
20	indicates a disturbed mind
21	He says that worries will keep old men awake. The CONTRAST between youth and AGE is again emphasized
22	not damaged by the world
23	uneasiness

FRIAR LAWRENCE God pardon sin! *(1)* wast thou with Rosaline? **45**
ROMEO With Rosaline, my *(2)* ghostly father? no;
   I have forgot that name, and that *(3)* name's woe.
FRIAR LAWRENCE That's my good son: but where hast thou been, then?
ROMEO I'll tell thee ere thou ask it me again.
   I have been feasting with mine enemy; **50**
   Where, on a sudden, one hath *(4)* wounded me
   That's by me wounded; both our *(5)* remedies
   (6) Within thy help and holy physic lies:
   I bear no hatred, blessed man; for, lo,
   My *(7)* intercession likewise *(8)* steads my foe. **55**
FRIAR LAWRENCE Be plain, good son, and *(9)* homely in thy drift;
   Riddling confession finds but riddling *(10)* shrift.
ROMEO Then plainly know my heart's dear love is set
   On the fair daughter of rich Capulet:
   As mine on hers, so hers is set on mine; **60**
   And all *(11)* combin'd, *(12)* save what thou must combine
   By holy marriage: when, and where, and how
   We met, we woo'd, and made exchange of vow,
   I'll tell thee *(13)* as we pass; but this I pray,
   That thou consent to marry us to-day. **65**
FRIAR LAWRENCE *(14)* Holy St. Francis! what a change is here!
   Is Rosaline, whom thou didst love so dear,
   So soon forsaken? young men's love, then, lies
   Not truly *(15)* in their hearts, but in their eyes.
   Jesu Maria, what a *(16)* deal of brine **70**
   Hath wash'd thy *(17)* sallow cheeks for Rosaline!
   How much *(18)* salt water thrown away in waste,
   To season love, that of it *(19)* doth not taste!
   The sun not yet thy sighs from heaven clears,
   Thy old groans ring yet in my ancient ears; **75**
   Lo, here upon thy cheek the stain doth sit
   Of an old tear that is not wash'd off yet:
   If e'er thou wast thyself, and these woes thine,
   Thou and these woes were all for Rosaline:
   And art thou chang'd? pronounce this *(20)* sentence, then, – **80**
   Women may fall, when there's no strength in men.
ROMEO Thou *(21)* chidd'st me oft for loving Rosaline.
FRIAR LAWRENCE For doting, not for loving, pupil mine.
ROMEO And bad'st me bury love.
FRIAR LAWRENCE   *(22)* Not in a grave, **85**
   To lay one in, another out to have.

Notes:

1. Friar Lawrence immediately worries that Romeo has committed the sin of impurity
2. holy
3. misery associated with her
4. wounded by Cupid's arrow, as she has been also
5. the remedy for both of us
6. your ability to marry us
7. request
8. benefits
9. straight forward
10. absolution, forgiveness
11. united
12. except
13. as we walk along
14. Lawrence is a Franciscan
15. they are attracted by superficial beauty
16. salt water (tears)
17. pale
18. tears
19. still has no flavour
20. saying
21. rebuked
22. despite the IRONIC humour here in Lawrence's genuine surprise, there is an element of PREMONITION

ROMEO I pray thee, chide not: she whom I love now
    Doth grace for grace and love for love allow;
    The other did not so.
FRIAR LAWRENCE *(1)* O, she knew well   90
    Thy love did read by rote, and could not spell.
    But come, young waverer, come, go with me,
    In one *(2)* respect I'll thy assistant be;
    (3) For this alliance may so happy prove,
    To turn your households' *(4)* rancour to pure love.   95
ROMEO O, let us hence; I *(5)* stand on sudden haste.
FRIAR LAWRENCE Wisely and slow; they stumble that run fast.

                                    (Exeunt.

ACT TWO, SCENE FOUR
A STREET.

Enter BENVOLIO *and* MERCUTIO.

MERCUTIO Where the devil *(6)* should this Romeo be? –
    Came he not home *(7)* to-night?
BENVOLIO Not to his father's; I spoke with his *(8)* man.
MERCUTIO *(9)* Ah, that same pale hard-hearted wench, that Rosaline,
    Torments him so that he will sure run mad.   5
BENVOLIO Tybalt, the kinsman of old Capulet,
    Hath sent a letter to his father's house.
MERCUTIO A challenge, on my life.
BENVOLIO Romeo will *(10)* answer it.
MERCUTIO *(11)* Any man that can write may answer a letter.   10
BENVOLIO Nay, he will answer the letter's master, how he *(12)* dares,
    being *(13)* dared.
MERCUTIO Alas, poor Romeo, he is already dead!
    (14) stabbed with a white wench's black eye; shot through the ear
    with a love-song; the very *(15)* pin of his heart cleft with *(16)* the   15
    blind bow-boy's *(17)* butt-shaft: and *(18)* is he a man to encounter
    Tybalt?
BENVOLIO Why, what is Tybalt?
MERCUTIO More than *(19)* prince of cats, I can tell you.
    O, he is the courageous *(20)* captain of compliments.   20
    He fights as you sing *(21)* prick-song, keeps time, distance, and
    proportion; *(22)* rests me his minim rest, one, two, and the third in
    your bosom; the *(23)* very butcher of a silk button, a duellist, a

---

Side notes:

1 Rosaline was wise enough to know that it was a pretended love, as a child who cannot read learns passages by heart to fool others
2 for one reason
3 Lawrence will help them to bring about LOVE from ENMITY. The DRAMATIC IRONY is that it will only be by their deaths.
4 ill-will
5 insist
6 can
7 last night
8 servant
9 Mercutio is unaware of the change in Romeo's affections
10 accept the challenge
11 Mercutio deliberately PUNS as does Benvolio below
12 is willing to fight
13 challenged to
14 Mercutio uses the ARROW image
15 bull's eye
16 Cupid
17 arrow
18 Mercutio jokes about Romeo being as useless as if he were dead because of lovesickness, but the DRAMATIC IRONY is bitter.
19 Tybalt was a legendary cat's name
20 best at duelling etiquette, cf Benvolio's account in Act 1, Scene 1
21 written on a song sheet
22 he fights as if to a musical score
23 his aim is perfect

duellist; a gentleman of [1] the very first house, – of the first and
second cause: ah, the immortal [2] passado! the punto reverso! the   25
hay! –

BENVOLIO The what?

MERCUTIO The [3] pox of such [4] antic, lisping, [5] affecting fantasticoes;
these new tuners of [6] accents! –

By Jesu, a very good blade! – a very tall man! – a very good   30
whore! – Why, is not this a lamentable thing, [7] grandsire, that we
should be thus afflicted with these strange [8] flies, these fashion-
mongers, these *pardonnez-mois,* [9] who stand so much on the new
form that they cannot sit at ease on the old bench? O, their *bons,*
their *bons!*   35

BENVOLIO Here comes Romeo, here comes Romeo.

MERCUTIO Without his roe, like a dried herring, – O, flesh, flesh, how
art thou [10] fishified! – Now is he for [11] the numbers that
Petrarch flowed, in: [12] Laura, to his lady, was but a kitchen-
wench, – marry, she had a better love to be-rhyme her: [13] Dido, a   40
dowdy; Cleopatra, a gipsy; Helen and Hero, hildings and harlots;
Thisbe, a gray eye or so, but not to the purpose, –

Enter ROMEO.

Signior Romeo, bon jour! there's a French salutation to your
French [14] slop. You gave us the [15] counterfeit fairly last night.

ROMEO Good-morrow to you both. What counterfeit did I give you?   45

MERCUTIO The slip, sir, the slip; can you not [16] conceive?

ROMEO Pardon, good Mercutio, my business was great; and in such a
case as mine a man may strain courtesy.

MERCUTIO That's as much as to say, such a case as yours constrains a
man to [17] bow in the hams.   50

ROMEO Meaning, to court'sy.

MERCUTIO Thou hast most kindly hit it.

ROMEO A most courteous exposition.

MERCUTIO Nay, I am the very [18] pink of courtesy.

ROMEO Pink for flower.   55

MERCUTIO Right.

ROMEO Why, then is my [19] pump well flowered.

MERCUTIO Well said: follow me this jest now till thou hast worn out thy
[20] pump; that when the single sole of it is worn, the jest may
remain, after the wearing, sole singular.   60

ROMEO O [21] single-soled jest, solely singular for the [22] singleness!

MERCUTIO [23] Come between us, good Benvolio; my wits faint.

ROMEO [24] Switch and spurs, switch and spurs; or [25] I'll cry a match.

---

1 finest fencing academy
2 fencing terms
3 plague
4 absurd
5 affected fops
6 fashionable language
7 Mercutio is teasing the serious Benvolio
8 parasites who indulge in affected phrases
9 they are so particular about seeming modern that they complain about everything old. There is a PUN on form and bench
10 presumably this has something to do with his PUN on Romeo's name - herring roe
11 SONNET form (The IRONY is that Romeo is far beyond his previous love-sickness and all that went with it)
12 Laura was the subject of Petrarch's sonnets. Mercutio suggest that without the poet she would never have been heard of.
13 the following are famous lovers, Mercutio satirizes them
14 a reference to Romeo's baggy breeches
15 slip
16 understand
17 curtsey (PUN in courtesy, below)
18 height
19 shoes (pumps) were decorated with holes - pinking
20 shoe
21 thin
22 silliness
23 DRAMATIC IRONY - Romeo comes between him and Tybalt, causing his death
24 an expression used to urge horses on, here referring to wit
25 claim that I have won

MERCUTIO Nay, if thy wits run the wild-goose chase, I have done; for
thou hast more of the wild-goose in one of thy wits than, I am   65
sure, I have in my whole five: was I with you *(1)* there for the goose?

ROMEO Thou wast never with me for anything when thou wast not
there for *(2)* the goose.

MERCUTIO I will *(3)* bite thee by the ear for that jest.

ROMEO Nay, good goose, bite not.   70

MERCUTIO Thy wit is a very bitter *(4)* sweeting; it is a most sharp *(5)* sauce.

ROMEO And is it not well served in to a sweet goose?

MERCUTIO O, here's a wit of *(6)* cheveril, that stretches from an inch
narrow to an *(7)* ell broad!

ROMEO I stretch it out for that word, broad: which added to the goose,   75
proves thee far and wide a *(8)* broad goose.

MERCUTIO Why, is not this better now than groaning for love? now art
thou sociable, now art thou Romeo; not art thou what thou art,
by *(9)* art as well as by nature: for this drivelling love is like a great
(10) natural, that runs lolling up and down to hide his *(11)* bauble in   80
a hole.

BENVOLIO Stop there, stop there.

MERCUTIO Thou desirest me to stop in my tale *(12)* against the hair.

BENVOLIO *(13)* Thou wouldst else have made thy tale large.

MERCUTIO O, thou art deceived; I would have made it short: for I was   85
come to the whole depth of my tale; and meant, indeed, to
(14) occupy the argument no longer.

ROMEO Here's goodly *(15)* gear!

Enter Nurse *and* PETER.

MERCUTIO *(16)* A sail, a sail, a sail!

BENVOLIO Two, two; *(17)* a shirt and a smock.   90

NURSE Peter!

PETER Anon?

NURSE My fan, Peter.

MERCUTIO Good Peter, to hide her face; for her fan's *(18)* the fairer face.

NURSE *(19)* God ye good-morrow, gentlemen.   95

MERCUTIO God ye good-den, fair gentlewoman.

NURSE Is it good-den?

MERCUTIO 'Tis no less, I tell you; for the bawdy hand of the dial is now
upon the *(20)* prick of noon.

NURSE Out upon you! what a man are you!   100

ROMEO One, gentlewoman, that God hath made himself to mar.

NURSE *(21)* By my troth, it is well said; – for himself to mar, quoth 'a? –
Gentlemen, can any of you tell me where I may find the young

---

1 Have I scored in this silly
business?

2 to play the fool

3 an affectionate threat

4 a sweet apple

5 sweet meat needs a sharp
sauce

6 stretchy leather, probably
kid

7 45 inches, 1143mm

8 indecent fool

9 by education (art) and by
birth (nature)

10 idiot

11 a fools' stick (bawdy
innuendo)

12 unwillingly

13 obscene PUN

14 "occupy" was an indecent
word

15 matter for amusement

16 cf "ship ahoy" - the nurse
is probably over-dressed

17 a man and a woman

18 the prettier of the two

19 good day

20 point (she has taken
three hours to find him)

21 upon my word

Romeo?

ROMEO I can tell you: but young Romeo will be older when you have 105
found him than he was when you sought him: I am the youngest
of that name, for *(1)* fault of a worse.

NURSE You say well.

MERCUTIO Yea, is the worst well? very well took, i' faith; *(2)* wisely, wisely.

NURSE If you be he, sir, I desire some *(3)* confidence with you. 110

BENVOLIO She will *(4)* indite him to some supper.

MERCUTIO A *(5)* bawd, a bawd, a bawd! So ho!

ROMEO What hast thou found?

MERCUTIO No *(6)* hare, sir; unless a hare, sir, in *(7)* a lenten pie, that is
something stale and *(8)* hoar ere it be *(9)* spent.   *(Sings.* 115

An old hare hoar,
And an old hare hoar,
Is very good meat in Lent:
But a hare that is hoar
Is *(10)* too much for a score,   120
When it hoars ere it be spent.

Romeo, will you come to your father's? we'll to dinner thither.

ROMEO I will follow you.

MERCUTIO Farewell, *(11)* ancient lady; farewell, – *(Singing)* lady, lady, lady.
                              (Exeunt MERCUTIO *and* BENVOLIO

NURSE Marry, farewell! – I pray you, sir, what *(12)* saucy merchant was 125
this, that was so full of his *(13)* ropery?

ROMEO A gentleman, nurse, that loves to hear himself talk; and will
speak more in a minute than he will *(14)* stand to in a month.

NURSE An 'a speak anything against me, I'll *(15)* take him down, an 'a
were lustier than he is, and twenty such *(16)* Jacks; and if I cannot, 130
I'll find those that shall. Scurvy knave! I am none of his *(17)* flirt-
gills; I am none of his *(18)* skainsmates. – And thou must stand by
too, and *(19)* suffer every knave to use me at his pleasure?

PETER I saw no man use you *(20)* at his pleasure; if I had, my weapon
should quickly have been out, I warrant you: I dare draw as soon 135
as another man, if I see *(21)* occasion in a *(22)* good quarrel, and the
law on my side.

NURSE Now, afore God, I am so vexed that every part about me quivers.
Scurvy knave! – Pray you, sir, a word: and as I told you, my young
lady bade me inquire you out; what she bade me say I will keep to 140
myself: but first let me tell ye, if ye should *(23)* lead her into a
fool's paradise, as they say, it were a very *(24)* gross kind of

1	there not being a worse
2	because she has pretended to understand Romeo's quibble
3	conference, discussion (she has used the wrong word)
4	invite - Benvolio is mocking her misuse of words
5	brothel-keeper
6	prostitute
7	a pie without meat - tasteless
8	mouldy
9	eaten
10	not good enough to be paid for
11	old (their rudeness to the Nurse is outrageous!)
12	impudent
13	bawdy talk
14	carry out
15	humble him
16	rascals
17	loose women
18	rascally companions
19	allow
20	bawdy pun
21	reason
22	legitimate
23	deceive her
24	monstrous

behaviour, as they say: for the gentlewoman is young; and,
therefore, if you should (1) deal double with her, truly it were an ill
thing to be offered to any gentlewoman, and very (2) weak dealing. 145

ROMEO Nurse, commend me to thy lady and mistress. I (3) protest unto
thee, –

NURSE Good heart, and, i' faith, (4) I will tell her as much: Lord, Lord,
she will be a joyful woman.

ROMEO What wilt thou tell her, nurse? thou dost not (5) mark me. 150

NURSE I will tell her, sir, – that you do protest; which, as I take it, is a
gentlemanlike offer.

ROMEO <u>Bid her devise some means to come to (6) shrift</u>
<u>This afternoon;</u>
<u>And there she shall at Friar Lawrence' cell</u> 155
<u>Be (7) shriv'd and married.</u> (8) Here is for thy pains.

NURSE No, truly, sir; not a penny.

ROMEO Go to; I say you shall.

NURSE. This afternoon, sir? well, she shall be there.

ROMEO And stay, good nurse, behind the abbey-wall: 160
Within this hour my man shall be with thee,
And bring thee cords made like (9) a tackled stair;
Which to the high (10) top-gallant of my joy
Must be my (11) convoy in the secret night.
Farewell; be (12) trusty, and I'll (13) quit thy pains: 165
Farewell; commend me to thy mistress.

NURSE Now God in heaven bless thee! –
Hark you, sir.

ROMEO What say'st thou, my dear nurse?

NURSE Is your man (14) secret? Did you ne'er hear say 170
Two may keep counsel, putting (15) one away?

ROMEO I (16) warrant thee, my man's as true as steel.

NURSE Well, sir; my mistress is the sweetest lady, – Lord, Lord! when
'twas a little prating thing, – O, there's a nobleman in town, one
Paris, that would (17) fain lay knife aboard; but she, good soul, had 175
as (18) lief see a toad, a very toad, as see him. I anger her sometimes,
and tell her that Paris is the (19) properer man; but, I'll warrant
you, when I say so, she looks as pale as any (20) clout in the
(21) versal world. Doth not rosemary and Romeo begin both with a
letter? 180

ROMEO Ay, nurse; what of that? both with an R.

NURSE Ah, mocker! that's the dog's name. R is for the dog: no; (22) I
know it begins with some other letter: – and she hath the
prettiest (23) sententious of it, of you and (24) rosemary, that it

1	double cross
2	contemptible
3	swear
4	i.e. that he "protests", swears his love
5	listen to
6	confession
7	confessed (before the sacrament of marriage)
8	Romeo offers her payment
9	a rope ladder
10	the highest sail on a ship (Romeo again associates himself with the sea)
11	conveyance (i.e. the rope ladder as in climbing rigging)
12	faithful
13	reward your trouble
14	able to keep a secret
15	two can keep a secret but not a third
16	promise
17	wish to stake his claim to his place by putting his knife on the table
18	would rather
19	more handsome
20	dish cloth
21	universal, whole
22	she is illiterate
23	she is using the wrong word again, she means "sayings"
24	to do with weddings

would do you good to hear it.   185

ROMEO Commend me to thy lady.

NURSE Ay, a thousand times.   (*Exit* ROMEO.

– Peter!

PETER Anon?

NURSE Peter, take my fan and *(1)* go before.   (*Exeunt.* 190   *1* go in front of me

ACT TWO, SCENE FIVE

CAPULET'S GARDEN.

Enter JULIET.

JULIET The clock struck nine when I did send the nurse;   *2* perhaps

In half an hour she promis'd to return.   *3* messengers carrying

(2) Perchance she cannot meet him: – that's not so. –   lovers' thoughts should

O, she is lame! *(3)* love's heralds should be thoughts,   be faster than light

Which ten times faster glide than the sun's beams   5   *4* DARK and threatening

Driving back shadows over *(4)* lowering hills: (N.B. LIGHT "sun's

Therefore do *(5)* nimble-pinion'd doves draw *(6)* love,   beams" dispenses

And therefore hath the wind-swift Cupid wings.   darkness, cf Sonnet 66)

Now is the sun *(7)* upon the highmost hill   *5* swift winged

Of this day's journey; and from nine till twelve   10   *6* the chariot of Venus,

Is three long hours, – yet she is not come.   goddess of love, was

(8) Had she *(9)* affections and warm youthful blood,   drawn by doves

She'd be as swift in motion as a ball;   *7* at its zenith

My words would *(10)* bandy her to my sweet love,   *8* Juliet is complaining of

And his to me: 15   her nurse's age being an

But old folks, many *(11)* feign as they were dead;   impediment to speed

Unwieldy, slow, heavy and pale as lead. –   *9* feelings

O God, she comes!   *10* go back and forth as in

                                                                         tennis

Enter NURSE *and* PETER.   *11* act as if they were dead

O *(12)* honey nurse, what news?   *12* contrast in her tone here,

Hast thou met with him? Send thy man away.   20   the nurse is suddenly a

NURSE Peter, stay at the gate.   sweet thing instead of

                                        (*Exit* PETER.   something half dead

JULIET Now, good sweet nurse, – O Lord, why look'st thou sad?

Though news be sad, yet tell *(13)* them merrily;   *13* items of news

If good, thou sham'st the music of sweet news   25

By playing it to me with so sour a face.

NURSE I am a-weary, give me leave a-while; –

Fie, how my bones ache! what a jaunt have I had!

JULIET I would thou hadst my bones and I thy news:

Nay, come, I pray thee, speak; – good, good nurse, speak.   30

NURSE Jesu, what haste? can you not *(2)* stay awhile?

Do you not see that I am out of breath?

JULIET How art thou out of breath, when thou hast breath

To say to me that thou art out of breath?

The excuse that thou dost make in this delay   35

Is longer than the tale thou dost excuse.

Is thy news good or bad? answer to that;

Say either, and I'll *(3)* stay the circumstance:

Let me be satisfied, is't good or bad?

NURSE *(4)* Well, you have made a *(5)* simple choice; you know not how to   40

choose a man: Romeo! no, not he; though his face be better than

any man's, yet his leg excels all men's; and for a hand, and a foot,

and a body, – though *(6)* they be not to be talked on, yet they are

past compare: he is not the flower of courtesy, – but I'll warrant

him as gentle as a lamb. – *(7)* Go thy ways, wench; serve God. –   45

What, have you dined at home?

Juliet No, no: but all this did I know before.

What, says he of our marriage? what of that?

NURSE Lord, how my head aches! what a head have I!

It beats as it would fall in twenty pieces.   50

My back *(8)* o' t' other side, – O, my back, my back! –

(9) Beshrew your heart for sending me about

To catch my death with jaunting up and down!

JULIET I' faith, I am sorry that thou art not well.

Sweet, sweet, sweet nurse, tell me, what says my love?   55

NURSE Your love says, like an honest gentleman,

And a courteous, and a kind, and a handsome,

And, I warrant, a virtuous, – Where is your mother?

JULIET Where is my mother! – why, she is within:

Where should she be? How oddly thou repliest!   60

Your love says, like an honest gentleman, –

Where is your mother?

NURSE   O *(10)* God's lady dear!

Are you so *(11)* hot! *(12)* marry, come up, I trow;

Is this the poultice of my aching bones?   65

Henceforward, do your messages yourself.

JULIET Here's such a *(13)* coil! – come, what says Romeo?

NURSE Have you got leave to go to shrift today?

JULIET I have.

---

1 Juliet IRONICALLY states that she would swap youth for age

2 wait

3 wait for details

4 IRONY - she is teasing Juliet

5 foolish

6 they are not worth talking about

7 enough of that

8 possibly Juliet is rubbing it

9 confound

10 our lady (mother of Christ)

11 angry

12 exclamation, pretending to be offended

13 fuss

NURSE Then [1] hie you hence to Friar Lawrence' cell;   70
    There stays a husband to make you a wife:
    Now comes the [2] wanton blood up in your cheeks,
    They'll be in [3] scarlet straight at any news.
    [4] Hie you to church; I must another way,
    To fetch a ladder, by the which your love   75
    Must climb a [5] bird's nest soon when it is dark:
    I am the drudge, and toil in your delight;
    But you shall [6] bear the burden soon at night.
    Go; I'll to dinner; hie you to the cell.
JULIET [7] Hie to high fortune! – honest nurse, farewell.   *(Exeunt.*   80

ACT TWO, SCENE SIX
FRIAR LAWRENCE'S CELL.

Enter FRIAR LAWRENCE *and* ROMEO.

FRIAR LAWRENCE [8] So smile the heavens upon this holy act
    That after-hours with sorrow chide us not!
ROMEO Amen, amen! [9] but come what sorrow can,
    It cannot [10] countervail the exchange of joy
    That one short minute gives me in her sight: 5
    Do thou but close our hands with holy words,
    [11] Then love-devouring death do what he dare, –
    It is enough I may but call her mine.
FRIAR LAWRENCE These violent delights have violent ends,
    And in their triumph die; [12] like fire and powder,   10
    Which, as they kiss, consume: the [13] sweetest honey
    Is loathsome in his own deliciousness,
    And in the taste confounds the appetite:
    Therefore love moderately; [14] long love doth so;
    Too swift arrives as [15] tardy as too slow.   15
    Here comes the lady. – O, so light a foot
    Will [16] ne'er wear out the everlasting flint:
    A lover may bestride the [17] gossamer
    That idles in the [18] wanton summer air
    And yet not fall; so light is [19] vanity.   20

    Enter JULIET.
JULIET Good-even to my [20] ghostly confessor.
FRIAR LAWRENCE Romeo shall thank thee, daughter, for us both.

---

1   go quickly
2   uncontrolled
3   blushing (there are several references to Juliet's tendency to blush)
4   hurry
5   to Juliet's room
6   i.e. in love making; the nurse cannot resist a bawdy reference
7   IRONIC PUN - her fortune will be the reverse
8   let the heavens approve of this marriage
9   let whatever sorrow come what may
10   outweigh
11   IRONY because the PREMONITION of death is correct
12   the first use of the GUNPOWDER image
13   sweet things can become sickly and therefore loathsome
14   IRONY, they will not have the chance to put it to the test
15   i.e. because accidents can occur to hold up the hasty
16   Juliet is as if she is walking on air
17   cobwebs
18   playful
19   empty joys on this earth as opposed to heavenly joy
20   holy

JULIET As much to him, else is his ⁽¹⁾ thanks too much.		1 i.e. his kiss, which he
ROMEO Ah, Juliet, if the measure of thy joy		gives her
Be heap'd like mine, and ⁽²⁾ that thy skill be more	25	2 and if
To ⁽³⁾ blazon it, then sweeten with thy breath		3 describe
This neighbour air, and let ⁽⁴⁾ rich music's tongue		4 your sweet voice

JULIET As much to him, else is his *(1)* thanks too much.
ROMEO Ah, Juliet, if the measure of thy joy
    Be heap'd like mine, and *(2)* that thy skill be more   25
    To *(3)* blazon it, then sweeten with thy breath
    This neighbour air, and let *(4)* rich music's tongue
    Unfold the *(5)* imagin'd happiness that both
    Receive *(6)* in either by this dear *(7)* encounter.
JULIET *(8)* Conceit, more rich in matter than in words,   30
    (9) Brags of his *(10)* substance, not of ornament:
    They are but *(11)* beggars that can count their worth;
    But my true love is grown to *(12)* such excess,
    I cannot *(13)* sum up half my sum of wealth.
FRIAR LAWRENCE Come, come with me, and we will make short work;   35
    For, by your leaves, you shall not *(14)* stay alone
    Till holy church *(15)* incorporate two in one.   *(Exeunt.*

ACT THREE, SCENE ONE
A PUBLIC PLACE.

Enter MERCUTIO, BENVOLIO, Page, *and* Servants.

BENVOLIO *(16)* I pray thee, good Mercutio, let's retire:
    The day is hot, the Capulets abroad,
    (17) And, if we meet, we shall not scape a brawl;
    For now, these hot days, is the mad blood stirring.
MERCUTIO Thou art like one of those fellows that, when he enters the   5
    confines of a tavern, claps me his sword upon the table, and says,
    (18) *God send me no one of thee!* and by the *(19)* operation of the
    second cup *(20)* draws it on the drawer, when, indeed, there is no
    need.
BENVOLIO Am I like such a fellow?   10
MERCUTIO Come, come, thou art as hot a *(21)* Jack in thy mood as any in
    Italy; and as soon *(22)* moved to be moody, and as soon moody to
    be *(23)* moved.
BENVOLIO And what to?
MERCUTIO Nay, an there were *(24)* two such, we should have none shortly,   15
    for one would kill the other. Thou! why, thou wilt quarrel with a
    man that hath a hair more or a hair less in his beard than thou
    hast. Thou wilt quarrel with a man for cracking nuts, having no

Notes:
1 i.e. his kiss, which he gives her
2 and if
3 describe
4 your sweet voice
5 anticipated
6 from each other
7 meeting
8 understanding
9 boasts
10 what is real and does not embellish it with exaggerated words. (Juliet is a much more practical lover than Romeo)
11 i.e. because they have not much wealth to count
12 I have so much
13 add it up, she PUNS on the verb and the noun
14 stay here alone
15 i.e. marries you
16 Benvolio is the peacemaker again
17 Note the contrast with what has just occurred
18 "I am not going to use my sword"
19 by the time he has had a second drink
20 draws his sword on the servant (N.B. PUN)
21 fellow
22 inclined to anger (N.B. there is no evidence in this play for this)
23 angry at being provoked
24 PUN on "to" above

other reason but because thou hast hazel eyes; – what eye but
such an eye would spy out such a quarrel? Thy head is as full of   20
quarrels as an egg is full of *(1)* meat; and yet thy head hath been
beaten as *(2)* addle as an egg for quarrelling. Thou hast quarrelled
with a man for coughing in the street, because he hath wakened
thy dog that hath lain asleep in the sun. Didst thou not fall out
with a tailor for wearing his new *(3)* doublet before Easter? with   25
another for tying his new shoes with old *(4)* riband? and yet thou
wilt tutor me from quarrelling!

BENVOLIO An I were so apt to quarrel as thou art, any man should buy
the *(5)* fee-simple of my life *(6)* for an hour and a quarter.

MERCUTIO The fee-simple! O *(7)* simple!   30

BENVOLIO *(8)* By my head, here come the Capulets.

MERCUTIO *(9)* By my heel, I care not.

Enter TYBALT *and others*.

TYBALT Follow me close, for I will speak to them. – Gentlemen, good-
den: a word with one of you.

MERCUTIO And but one word with one of us?   35
    (10) Couple it with something; make it a word and a blow.

TYBALT You shall find me apt enough to that, sir, an you will give me
    (11) occasion.

MERCUTIO Could you not take some occasion without giving?

TYBALT Mercutio, thou consort'st with Romeo, –   40

MERCUTIO *(12)* Consort! what, dost thou make us minstrels? An thou
    make minstrels of us, look to hear nothing but discords: here's
    my *(13)* fiddlestick; here's that shall make you dance.
    Zounds, consort!

BENVOLIO We talk here in the public haunt of men: 45
    Either withdraw unto some private place,
    And *(14)* reason coldly of your grievances,
    Or else *(15)* depart; here all eyes gaze on us.

MERCUTIO Men's eyes were made to look, and let them gaze;
    I will not budge for no man's pleasure, I.   50

TYBALT Well, peace with you, sir. Here comes *(16)* my man.

Enter ROMEO.

MERCUTIO But I'll be hanged, sir, if he *(17)* wear your livery:
    Marry, go before *(18)* to field, he'll be your follower;
    Your worship in that sense may call him *(19)* man.

TYBALT Romeo, the *(20)* hate I bear thee can afford   55
    No better term than this, – Thou art a villain.

1   food

2   rotten

3   jacket (Easter was the
     time for showing off new
     clothes)

4   ribbon

5   absolute possession

6   he means, "I would not
     last that long"

7   stupid

8   On my life

9   he will not run away

10 N.B. Mercutio is not a
     Montague but he is being
     provocative

11 excuse

12 He takes it in the sense of
     playing in harmony.
     Musicicans/minstrels
     were servants - it is
     taken as an insult.

13 sword

14 discuss calmly

15 part company

16 i.e. Romeo

17 is your servant (by
     wearing his uniform,
     livery)

18 the duelling place

19 courageous. (All the
     PUNS are on the different
     meanings of man)

20 The folio text has "love",
     but as irony is not typical
     of Tybalt, the Quanto's
     "hate" is better

ROMEO <u>Tybalt, the reason that I have to</u> ⁽¹⁾ <u>love thee</u>

Doth much excuse the appertaining ⁽²⁾ rage

To such a greeting. Villain am I none;

Therefore, farewell; I see thou know'st me not.   60

TYBALT ⁽³⁾ Boy, this shall not excuse the injuries

That thou hast done me; therefore turn and draw.

ROMEO I do protest I never injur'd thee;

But love thee better than thou canst ⁽⁴⁾ devise

Till thou shalt know the reason of my love: 65

And so, good Capulet, – which name I ⁽⁵⁾ tender

As dearly as my own. – be satisfied.

MERCUTIO O ⁽⁶⁾ calm, dishonourable, vile submission!

⁽⁷⁾ *Alla stoccata* carries it away.   *(Draws.*

Tybalt, you ⁽⁸⁾ rat-catcher, will you ⁽⁹⁾ walk?   70

TYBALT What wouldst thou have with me?

MERCUTIO Good king of cats, nothing but one of your nine lives; that I

mean to make bold withal, and, as you ⁽¹⁰⁾ shall use me hereafter,

⁽¹¹⁾ dry-beat the rest of the eight. Will you ⁽¹²⁾ pluck your sword out

of his pilcher by the ears? make haste, lest mine be about your   75

ears ere it be out.

TYBALT I am for you.   *(Drawing.*

ROMEO Gentle Mercutio, put thy rapier up.

MERCUTIO Come, sir, your ⁽¹³⁾ passado.   *(They fight.*

ROMEO Draw, Benvolio; beat down their weapons. –   80

Gentlemen, for shame, ⁽¹⁴⁾ forbear this outrage! –

Tybalt, – Mercutio, – the prince expressly hath

Forbidden ⁽¹⁵⁾ bandying in Verona streets. –

⁽¹⁶⁾ Hold, Tybalt! – good Mercutio. –

(Exeunt TYBALT *and his* Partizans.

MERCUTIO   I am hurt; –   85

A plague, o' both your houses! – I am ⁽¹⁷⁾ sped. –

Is he gone, and hath ⁽¹⁸⁾ nothing?

BENVOLIO   What, art thou hurt?

MERCUTIO Ay, ay, a ⁽¹⁹⁾ scratch, a scratch; marry, 'tis enough. –

Where is my page? – go, ⁽²⁰⁾ villain, fetch a surgeon.   *(Exit Page.*   90

ROMEO Courage, man; the hurt cannot be much.

MERCUTIO No, 'tis not so deep as a well, nor so wide as a church-door;

but 'tis enough, 'twill serve: ask for me to-morrow, and you shall

find me a ⁽²¹⁾ grave man. I am ⁽²²⁾ peppered, I warrant, for this world.

– A plague o' both your houses! – Zounds, a dog, a rat, a mouse, a   95

cat, to scratch a man to death! a braggart, a rogue, a villain, that

fights by the ⁽²³⁾ book of arithmetic! – ⁽²⁴⁾ Why the devil came you

---

1   i.e. his marriage (Note
    the ANTITHESIS with
    hate)

2   the rage which should be
    the response

3   Tybalt is being insulting

4   imagine

5   hold

6   mild

7   a fencing term for thrust

8   cf King of Cats

9   i.e. to find somewhere to
    fight

10 depending on your
    behaviour from there on

11 I shall beat you (without
    drawing blood)

12 the scabbard by the hilt

13 fencing term

14 cease

15 fighting

16 (At this point Romeo
    comes between them and
    Mercutio is wounded
    under his arm.)

17 speeding to my death

18 is he (Tybalt) not
    wounded?

19 the "scratch" is enough
    to kill him

20 term for a servant

21 Even though he is dying
    he can still play on words

22 finished

23 by the rules

24 It was purely by chance
    that Romeo should do
    this

between us? I was hurt under your arm.

ROMEO [1] I thought all for the best.

MERCUTIO Help me into some house, Benvolio,   100
    Or I shall faint. – A plague o' both your houses!
    They have made worm's meat of me:
    I have it, and soundly too. – Your houses!
                              (Exeunt MERCUTIO *and* BENVOLIO.

ROMEO This gentleman, the prince's [2] near ally,
    My very friend hath got his mortal hurt   105
    In my behalf; my reputation stain'd
    With Tybalt's [3] slander, – Tybalt, that an hour
    Hath been my [4] kinsman. – O sweet Juliet,
    Thy beauty hath made me effeminate,
    And in my [5] temper soften'd valour's steel.   110

Re-enter BENVOLIO.

BENVOLIO O Romeo, Romeo, brave Mercutio's dead!
    That gallant spirit hath [6] aspir'd the clouds
    Which too untimely here did scorn the earth.

ROMEO This day's black fate on more days doth depend;
    This but begins the woe others must end.   115

BENVOLIO Here comes the furious Tybalt back again.

ROMEO Alive, in triumph! and Mercutio slain!
    Away to heaven, respective lenity,
    And [7] fire-ey'd fury be my [8] conduct now! –

Re-enter TYBALT.

    Now, Tybalt, take the *villain* back again   120
    That [9] late thou gav'st me; for Mercutio's soul
    Is but a little way above our heads,
    [10] Staying for thine to keep him company:
    Either thou or I, or both, must [11] go with him.

TYBALT Thou, wretched boy, that didst [12] consort him here,   125
    Shalt with him hence.

ROMEO   [13] This shall determine that.
                              (They fight; TYBALT *falls.*

BENVOLIO Romeo, away, be gone!
    The citizens [14] are up, and Tybalt slain. –
    Stand not [15] amaz'd. The prince will [16] doom thee death   130
    If thou art taken. Hence, be gone, away!

ROMEO [17] O, I am fortune's fool!

BENVOLIO   Why dost thou stay?   *(Exit* ROMEO.

---

1 DRAMATIC IRONY, it was
   the worst thing he could
   do

2 kinsman

3 i.e. that he is a villain

4 he is Juliet's cousin

5 character (PUN on
   temper) made weak, not
   brave

6 in general terms: he has
   gone to heaven too soon
   having rejected material
   things on earth

7 fiery (Hellish)

8 guide

9 recently

10 waiting

11 i.e. to the death

12 accompany (like a low
    musician)

13 i.e. his sword

14 in arms

15 as in a daze

16 condemn, judge

17 the clown of fate -
    (Romeo is convinced that
    he is fated)

Enter Citizens, *& c.*

1 CITIZEN Which way ran he that kill'd Mercutio?

Tybalt, that murderer, which way ran he?   135

BENVOLIO There lies that Tybalt.

1 CITIZEN   *(1)* Up, sir, go with me;   *1* go along

I charge thee in the prince's name, obey.

Enter PRINCE, *attended;* MONTAGUE, CAPULET, *their* Wives *and others.*

PRINCE Where are the vile beginners of this fray?

BENVOLIO O noble prince, I can *(2)* discover all   140   *2* reveal

The unlucky *(3)* manage of this fatal brawl: *3* management

There lies the man, slain by young Romeo,

That slew thy kinsman, brave Mercutio.

LADY CAPULET Tybalt, my cousin! O my brother's child! –

O prince! – O husband! – O, the blood is spill'd   145

Of my dear kinsman! – Prince, as thou art true,

For blood of ours shed blood of Montague. –

O cousin, cousin!

PRINCE Benvolio, who began this bloody fray?

BENVOLIO Tybalt, here slain, whom Romeo's hand did slay;   150

Romeo that *(4)* spoke him fair, bade him bethink   *4* was respectful to him

How *(5)* nice the quarrel was, and *(6)* urg'd withal   *5* trivial

Your high displeasure. – All this, – uttered   *6* constantly reminded him

With gentle breath, calm look, knees humbly bow'd, –   of

Could not *(7)* take truce with the *(8)* unruly spleen   155   *7* make peace

Of Tybalt, deaf to peace, but that he *(9)* tilts   *8* uncontrollable temper of

With piercing steel at bold Mercutio's breast;   Tybalt

Who, all as hot, turns deadly point to point,   *9* thrusts

And, with a martial scorn, with one hand beats

Cold death aside, and with the other sends   160

It back to Tybalt, whose dexterity   *10* returns

(10) Retorts it: Romeo he cries aloud,

Hold, friends! friends, part! and, swifter than his tongue,   *11* blades

His agile arm beats down their fatal *(11)* points,

And 'twixt them rushes; underneath whose arm   165   *12* hateful

And *(12)* envious thrust from Tybalt hit the life

Of stout Mercutio, and then Tybalt fled: *13* immediately

But *(13)* by and by comes back to Romeo,   *14* only then thought of

Who had but *(14)* newly entertain'd revenge,

And to't they go like lightning; for ere I   170

Could draw to part them was stout Tybalt slain;

And as he fell did Romeo turn and fly.

This is the truth, or let Benvolio die.

LADY CAPULET He is a kinsman to the Montague,

(1) Affection makes him false, he speaks *(2)* not true: 175

Some *(3)* twenty of them fought in this black strife,

And all those twenty could but kill one life.

I beg for justice, which thou, prince, must give;

Romeo slew Tybalt, Romeo must not live.

PRINCE Romeo slew him, he slew Mercutio: 180

Who *(4)* now the price of his dear blood doth owe?

MONTAGUE Not Romeo, prince, he was Mercutio's friend;

(5) His fault concludes but what the law should end,

The life of Tybalt.

PRINCE   And for that offence,   185

Immediately we do exile him hence:

I have an interest in your hate's proceeding,

My *(6)* blood for your rude brawls doth lie a-bleeding;

But I'll *(7)* amerce you with so strong a fine

That you shall all repent the loss of mine: 190

I will be deaf to pleading and excuses;

Nor tears nor prayers shall *(8)* purchase out abuses,

Therefore use none: let Romeo hence in haste,

Else when he's found, that hour is his last.

Bear hence this body, and attend our will: 195

(9) Mercy but murders, pardoning those that kill.   *(Exeunt.*

ACT THREE, SCENE TWO
A ROOM IN CAPULET'S HOUSE.

Enter JULIET.

JULIET *(10)* Gallop apace, you *(11)* fiery-footed steeds,

Towards *(12)* Phœbus' *(13)* lodging; such a waggoner

As *(14)* Phaethon would whip you to the west,

And bring in cloudy night immediately. –

Spread thy *(15)* close curtain, *(16)* love-performing night!   5

That *(17)* rude day's eyes may wink, and Romeo

Leap to these arms, untalk'd of and unseen. –

(18) Lovers can see to do their amorous rites

By their own beauties: or if love be blind,

It best agrees with night. – Come, *(19)* civil night,   10

Thou sober-suited matron, all in black,

---

1 feeling

2 in fact, he has kept back Tybalt's provocation

3 Lady Capulet is now exaggerating

4 who will now pay the penalty of his death?

5 he did what the law would have done, he executed Tybalt (Montague is desperate to save his son from death)

6 Mercutio was his kinsman

7 punish

8 buy a pardon for crimes

9 being merciful to murderers encourages more

10 Juliet is longing for the LIGHT to go and DARKNESS to descend to allow her husband to come. (Ominous in that their future is DARK)

11 i.e. the horses pulling the chariot

12 God of the sun

13 where the sun sets (Phœbus' lodging)

14 Phœbus' son

15 i.e. to hide them

16 her marriage night

17 the Folio version has "rumour" which links with the line below

18 the idea of the lovers lighting the darkness with the radiance of their love is sustained. (N.B. the contrast LIGHT/DARK)

19 dark, as in the soberly dressed matron

And ⁽¹⁾ learn me how to ⁽²⁾ lose a winning match,
Play'd for a pair of stainless maidenhoods:
⁽³⁾ Hood my ⁽⁴⁾ unmann'd blood, ⁽⁵⁾ bating in my cheeks,
With thy black mantle; till ⁽⁶⁾ strange love, grown bold,   15
Think true love acted simple ⁽⁷⁾ modesty.
Come, night; – come, Romeo, – come, thou ⁽⁸⁾ day in night;
For thou wilt lie upon the wings of night
Whiter than new snow on a raven's back. –
Come, gentle night, – come, loving black-brow'd night,   20
Give me my Romeo; and, ⁽⁹⁾ when he shall die,
Take him and cut him out in little stars,
And he will make the face of heaven so fine
That all the world will be in love with night,
And pay no worship to the ⁽¹⁰⁾ garish sun, –   25
O, I have bought the mansion of a love,
But not possess'd it; and, though I am sold,
Not yet enjoy'd: so tedious is this day,
As is the night before some festival
To an impatient child that hath new ⁽¹¹⁾ robes,   30
And may not wear them. O, here comes my nurse,
⁽¹²⁾ And she brings news; and every tongue that speaks
But Romeo's name speaks heavenly eloquence. –

Enter Nurse *with* ⁽¹³⁾ *cords.*
Now, nurse, what news? What hast thou there? the cords
That Romeo bade thee fetch?   35

NURSE   Ay, ay, the cords. *(Throws them down.*
JULIET Ah me! what news? why dost thou wring thy hands?
NURSE Ah, well-a-day! he's dead, he's dead, he's dead,
    We are undone, lady, we are undone –
    Alack the day! – he's gone, he's kill'd, he's dead!   40
JULIET ⁽¹⁴⁾ Can heaven be so envious?
NURSE   Romeo ⁽¹⁵⁾ can,
    Though heaven cannot. – O Romeo, Romeo! –
    Who ever would have thought it? – Romeo –
JULIET ⁽¹⁶⁾ What devil art thou, that dost torment me thus?   45
    This torture should be roar'd in dismal hell.
    ⁽¹⁷⁾ Hath Romeo slain himself? say thou but ⁽¹⁸⁾ "Ay",
    And that bare vowel "I" shall poison more
    Than the death-darting eye of ⁽¹⁹⁾ cockatrice:
    "I" am not "I" if there by such an "I";   50
    Or ⁽²⁰⁾ those eyes shut that make thee answer "Ay".
    If he be slain, say "Ay"; or if not, "no";

1	teach
2	she will lose her maiden hood, but gain a husband
3	image from FALCONRY - hoods were used for inexperienced hawks to become used to men.
4	untamed, inexperienced
5	fluttering
6	modest, retiring
7	is chaste
8	Romeo, who lightens DARKNESS
9	DRAMATIC IRONY, because he is to die
10	bright
11	clothes
12	DRAMATIC IRONY - the news of Romeo is catastrophic, all the Capulets will speak against him
13	the rope ladder
14	so full of envy that it (fate) destroys them
15	i.e. to be envious
16	Juliet fears that there will be a repeat of the nurse's tactics in delaying the news of the wedding arrangements
17	her PREMONITION is accurate
18	Yes: even in moments of greatest stress Juliet uses a PUN
19	a legendary creature which could kill with a look
20	i.e. Romeo dead

Brief sounds determine of my weal or woe.

NURSE *(1)* I saw the wound, I saw it with mine eyes, –
God save the mark! – here on his manly breast:
A piteous *(2)* corse, a bloody piteous corse;
Pale, pale as ashes, all *(3)* bedaub'd in blood,
All in *(4)* gore-blood; – I swooned at the sight.

JULIET O, break, my heart! – poor *(5)* bankrupt, break at once!
(6) To prison, eyes, ne'er look on liberty!
(7) Vile earth, to earth resign; end motion here;
And thou and Romeo press one *(8)* heavy bier!

NURSE O Tybalt, Tybalt! the best friend I had!
O courteous Tybalt! honest gentleman!
That ever I should live to see thee dead!

JULIET What storm is this that blows so contrary?
Is Romeo slaughter'd, and is Tybalt dead?
My dear-lov'd cousin and my dearer lord? –
Then, dreadful trumpet, sound the *(9)* general doom!
For who is living if those two are gone?

NURSE Tybalt is gone, and Romeo banished;
Romeo that kill'd him, he is banished.

JULIET O God! – did Romeo's hand shed Tybalt's blood?

NURSE It did, it did; alas the day, it did!

JULIET O *(10)* serpent heart, *(11)* hid with a flowering face!
Did ever dragon keep so fair a *(12)* cave?
(13) Beautiful tyrant! fiend angelical!
Dove-feather'd raven! wolfish-ravening lamb!
Despised substance of divinest *(14)* show!
Just opposite to what thou *(15)* justly seem'st,
A damned saint, an honourable villain! –
O nature, what hadst thou to do in hell
When thou didst *(16)* bower the spirit of a fiend
In mortal paradise of such sweet flesh? –
(17) Was ever book containing such vile matter
So fairly bound? O, that deceit should dwell
In such a gorgeous palace!

NURSE   There's no trust,
No, faith, no honesty in men; all are perjur'd,
All forsworn, all *(18)* naught, all *(19)* dissemblers. –
Ah, where's my man? give me some *(20)* aqua vitae. –
These griefs, these woes, these sorrows make me old.
Shame come to Romeo!

JULIET   Blister'd be thy tongue

1	IRONY - she is talking about Tybalt
2	corpse
3	covered
4	gory
5	i.e. of Romeo's love
6	as a bankrupt
7	i.e. her body
8	sad
9	Judgement Day (the end of the world)
10	Satan
11	hidden by
12	i.e. guarding the treasure inside
13	ANTITHESIS - a series of balanced opposites follows
14	appearance
15	exactly
16	shelter
17	the IRONY is in the comparison with Lady Capulet's sustained image of Paris as a book, Act 1, Scene 3 line 84
18	wicked
19	liars
20	strong alcohol to revive her

For such a wish! <u>he was not born to shame:</u>
<u>Upon his brow shame is asham'd to sit;</u>   95
<u>For 'tis a throne where honour may be crown'd</u>
(1) <u>Sole monarch of the universal earth.</u>

     1 she probably means that his honour is the best in the world

O, what a beast was I to chide at him!

NURSE <u>Will you speak well of him that kill'd your cousin?</u>

JULIET <u>Shall I speak ill of him that is my husband?</u>   100
    Ah, poor my lord, what tongue shall *(2)* smooth thy name,
    When I, thy three-hours wife, have *(3)* mangled it? –
    But wherefore, *(4)* <u>villain, didst thou kill my cousin?</u>
    <u>That villain cousin would have kill'd my husband.</u>
    Back, foolish tears, back to your native spring;   105
    Your *(5)* tributary drops belong to *(6)* woe,
    Which you, mistaking, offer up to joy.
    My husband lives, that Tybalt would have slain;
    And Tybalt's dead that would have slain my husband:
    All this is comfort; wherefore weep I, then?   110
    Some word there was worser than Tybalt's death,
    That murder'd me: I would forget it *(7)* fain:
    But, O, it presses to my memory
    Like damned guilty deeds to sinners' minds:
    Tybalt is dead, and Romeo banished.   115
    That *banished,* that one word *banished,*
    Hath *(8)* slain ten thousand Tybalts. Tybalt's death
    Was woe enough, if it had ended there:
    Or, if sour woe delights in fellowship,
    And *(9)* needly will be rank'd with other griefs, –   120
    Why follow'd not, when she said Tybalt's dead,
    Thy father or thy mother, nay, or both,
    Which *(10)* modern lamentation might have mov'd?
    But, with a rear-ward following Tybalt's death,
    Romeo is banished, – to speak that word   125
    Is father, mother, Tybalt, Romeo, Juliet,
    All slain, all dead: *Romeo is banished,* –
    <u>There is no end, no limit, measure, bound.</u>
    <u>In that word's *(11)* death</u>; no words can that woe *(12)* sound. –
    Where is my father and my mother, nurse?   130

NURSE Weeping and wailing over Tybalt's corse:
    Will you go to them? I will bring you thither.

JULIET Wash they his wounds with tears: <u>mine shall be spent</u>
    <u>When theirs are dry, for Romeo's banishment.</u>
    Take up those cords. Poor ropes, you are *(13)* beguil'd,   135

2 smooth out the furrows in his reputation

3 disfigured (his reputation)

4 IRONY - in that she uses the exact word that Tybalt used

5 paying tribute to

6 sorrow

7 rather (she remembers "banished")

8 the word, constantly repeated, is 10,000 times worse than Tybalts' death

9 must be accompanied by

10 ordinary

11 it is death to her

12 measure the depths of that misery

13 deceived

Both you and I; for Romeo is exil'd:
He made you for a highway to my bed;
But I, a maid, die maiden-widowed.
Come, cords; come, nurse; I'll to my wedding-bed;
(1) And death, not Romeo, take my maidenhead!   140

NURSE Hie to your chamber, I'll find Romeo
To comfort you: I *(2)* wot well where he is.
Hark ye, your Romeo will be here at night:
I'll to him; he is hid at Lawrence' cell.

JULIET O, find him! give this ring to my true knight,   145
And bid him come to take his last farewell.   *(Exeunt.*

1	Juliet sees DEATH AS HER LOVER
2	know

ACT THREE, SCENE THREE

FRIAR LAWRENCE'S CELL.

Enter FRIAR LAWRENCE.

FRIAR LAWRENCE Romeo, come forth; come forth, thou *(3)* fearful man:
(4) Affliction is enamour'd of thy parts,
And thou art wedded to calamity.

3	full of fear
4	misery and calamity are now Romeo's lovers

Enter ROMEO.

ROMEO Father, what news? what is the prince's *(5)* doom?
What *(6)* sorrow craves acquaintance at my hand,   5
That I yet know not?

FRIAR LAWRENCE   *(7)* Too familiar
Is my dear son with such sour company:
I bring thee tidings of the prince's doom.

ROMEO What less than *(8)* doomsday is the prince's doom?   10

FRIAR LAWRENCE A gentler judgment *(9)* vanish'd from his lips,
Not body's death, but body's banishment.

ROMEO Ha, banishment! be merciful, say death;
For exile hath more terror in his look,
Much more than death: do not say banishment.   15

FRIAR LAWRENCE Hence from Verona art thou banish'd:
Be patient, for the world is broad and wide.

ROMEO There is no world *(10)* without Verona walls,
But purgatory, torture, hell itself.
Hence-banished is banish'd from the world,   20
And *(11)* world's exile is death, – then banished
Is death mis-term'd: calling death banishment,

5	judgement
6	personification of sorrow which wishes to be his companion
7	You are more than just the acquaintance of sorrow
8	Judgement Day (N B Romeo and Juliet use the same words and expressions)
9	on his breath perhaps?
10	outside of
11	to be exiled from the world

Thou cutt'st my head off with a golden axe,
And smil'st upon the stroke that murders me.

FRIAR LAWRENCE O (1) deadly sin! O rude unthankfulness!   25
(2) Thy fault our law calls death; but the kind prince,
Taking thy part, hath brush'd aside the law,
And turn'd that black word death to banishment:
This is (3) dear mercy, and thou see'st it not.

ROMEO 'Tis torture, and not mercy: <u>heaven is here</u>   30
<u>Where Juliet lives; and every cat, and dog,</u>
<u>And little mouse, every unworthy thing,</u>
<u>Live here in heaven, and may look on her</u>;
<u>But Romeo may not</u>. – More (4) validity,
More honourable state, more (5) <u>courtship</u> lives   35
In (6) carrion flies than Romeo: they may seize
On the white wonder of dear Juliet's hand,
And steel (7) immortal blessing from her lips;
Who, even in pure and (8) vestal modesty,
Still blush, as thinking their own (9) kisses sin;   40
But Romeo may not; he is banished, –
(10) This may <u>flies do</u>, when I from this must <u>fly</u>.
And say'st thou yet that exile is not death!
(11) Hadst thou no poison mix'd, no sharp-ground knife,
No sudden (12) <u>mean</u> of death, though ne'er so <u>mean</u>,   45
But – banished – to kill me; banished?
O friar, the damned use that word in hell;
Howlings attend it: how hast thou the heart,
Being a divine, a ghostly confessor,
A sin-absolver, and my friend profess'd,   50
To (13) mangle me with that word banishment?

FRIAR LAWRENCE Thou (14) fond mad man, hear me speak a little, –

ROMEO O, thou wilt speak again of banishment.

FRIAR LAWRENCE I'll give thee armour to keep off that word;
(15) Adversity's sweet milk, philosophy,   55
To comfort thee, though thou art banished.

ROMEO Yet banished? – (16) Hang up philosophy!
Unless philosophy can make a Juliet,
Displant a town, reverse a prince's doom,
It helps not, it prevails not, – talk no more.   60

FRIAR LAWRENCE O, then I see that madmen have (17) no ears.

ROMEO How should they, when that (18) wise men have no eyes?

FRIAR LAWRENCE Let me (19) dispute with thee of thy estate.

ROMEO Thou canst not speak of what (20) thou dost not feel:

1 sin of ingratitude
2 your offence is
    punishable by death

3 to be valued

4 value
5 PUN on courtier and <u>one</u>
    <u>who woos</u>
6 those who feed on flesh
7 he could mean heavenly
8 <u>chaste, virginal</u>
9 her lips blush when they
    meet each other
10 Just as Juliet used <u>PUNS</u>
    in the extremity of
    distress, so does Romeo
11 DRAMATIC IRONY in
    that he ultimately uses
    poison
12 PUN 1. means/ways.
    2. low/base
13 disfigure, mutilate.
    (Juliet used this word
    about his reputation)
14 foolish
15 philosophy is a comfort
    when in trouble
16 Romeo is still being
    ungrateful
17 will not listen
18 you, who are wise.
    cannot see the problem
    in banishment
19 discuss the state of affairs
20 cannot feel, because he is
    a celibate

Wert thou as young as I, Juliet thy love,   65

An hour but married, Tybalt murdered,

(1) Doting like me, and like me banished,   *1* loving extremely

Then mightst thou speak, then mightst thou tear thy hair,

And fall upon the ground, as I do now,

Taking the measure of an *(2)* unmade grave.   70   *2* DRAMATIC IRONY - he is

FRIAR LAWRENCE Arise; one knocks; good Romeo, hide thyself.   lying on the ground as if

                               (Knocking within.   measuring the length of

ROMEO Not I; unless the breath of *(3)* heart-sick groans,   his grave.

  Mist-like, enfold me from the search of eyes.   *(Knocking.*   *3* N.B. the repetition of the

FRIAR LAWRENCE Hark how they knock! – Who's there? – Romeo, arise;   image of sighs causing a

  Thou wilt be taken. – Stay awhile; – stand up;   *(Knocking.*   75   cloud of mist

  Run to my study. – *(4)* By and by. – God's will!   *4* "I am coming"

  What *(5)* simpleness is this! – I come, I come.   *(Knocking.*   *5* stupidity (i.e. he is still

  Who knocks so hard? whence come you? what's your will?   there, he has not hidden

NURSE *(Within.)* Let me come in and you shall know my errand;   himself)

  I come from Lady Juliet.   80

FRIAR LAWRENCE   Welcome, then.

Enter Nurse.

NURSE O holy friar, O, tell me, holy friar,

  Where is my lady's lord, where's Romeo?

FRIAR LAWRENCE There on the ground, with his own tears made drunk.

NURSE O, *(6)* he is even in my mistress' case, –   85   *6* they are acting in exactly

  Just in her case!   the same way

FRIAR LAWRENCE O woeful sympathy!

  (7) Piteous predicament!   *7* pitiful state of affairs

NURSE Even so lies she,

  Blubbering and weeping, weeping and blubbering. –   90

  Stand up, stand up; stand, an you be a man:

  For Juliet's sake, for her sake, rise and stand;

  Why should you fall into so deep an *(8)* O?   *8* the shape of his mouth

ROMEO Nurse!   when he is weeping,

NURSE   Ah, sir! ah, sir! – Well, death's the end of all.   95   coupled with the sound

ROMEO Spak'st thou of Juliet? how is it with her?   of his groaning

  Doth she not think me an *(9)* old murderer,   *9* practised

  Now I have stain'd the childhood of our joy

  With blood remov'd but little from her own?

  Where is she? and how doth she? and what says   100

  My *(10)* conceal'd lady to our *(11)* cancell'd love?   *10* unacknowledged wife

NURSE O, she says nothing, sir, but weeps and weeps;   *11* cancelled out by his

  And now falls on her bed; and then starts up,   crime

And Tybalt calls; and then on Romeo cries,
And then down falls again.   105
ROMEO   As if that name,
Shot from the deadly *(1)* level of a gun.
Did murder her; as that name's cursed hand
Murder'd her kinsman. – O, tell me, friar, tell me,
In what vile part of this *(2)* anatomy   110
Doth my name lodge? tell me that I may *(3)* sack
The hateful *(4)* mansion.   *(Drawing his sword.*
FRIAR LAWRENCE   Hold thy desperate hand:
Art thou a man? thy form cries out thou art:
Thy tears are womanish; thy wild acts denote   115
The unreasonable fury of a beast:
(5) Unseemly woman in a seeming man!
Or ill-beseeming beast in seeming *(6)* both!
Thou hast *(7)* amaz'd me: by my holy order,
I thought thy disposition better *(8)* temper'd.   120
Hast thou slain Tybalt? wilt thou slay thyself?
And slay thy lady, too, *(9)* that lives in thee,
By doing *(10)* damned hate upon thyself?
Why rail'st thou on thy birth, the heaven, and earth?
Since birth, and heaven and earth, all three do meet   125
In thee at once; which thou at once *(11)* wouldst lose.
Fie, fie! thou sham'st thy shape, thy love, thy wit:
Which, like a *(12)* usurer, abound'st in all,
And usest none in that true use indeed
Which should *(13)* bedeck thy shape, thy love, thy wit: 130
Thy noble shape is but a *(14)* form of wax,
(15) Digressing from the valour of a man;
Thy dear love sworn, but hollow perjury,
(16) Killing that love which thou hast vow'd to cherish;
Thy wit, that ornament to shape and love,   135
(17) Mis-shapen in the conduct of them *(18)* both,
(19) Like powder in a skilless soldier's flask,
Is set a-fire by thine own ignorance,
And thou *(20)* dismember'd with thine own defence.
What, rouse thee, man! thy Juliet is alive,   140
For whose dear sake thou wast but *(21)* lately dead;
There art thou happy: Tybalt would kill thee,
But thou slew'st Tybalt; there art thou happy too:
The law, that threaten'd death, becomes thy friend,
And turns it to exile; there art thou happy: 145

1   aim: (N.B. GUNPOWDER
    image)
2   body
3   wreck
4   his body. N.B. DRAMATIC
    IRONY in that he is again
    wanting to kill himself
    but also that he uses the
    very word Juliet used
    about his body Act 3,
    Scene 2, line 26
5   unnatural womanliness
    in you, who seem to be a
    man
6   i.e. man and woman (by
    indulging his emotions)
7   bewildered
8   balanced
9   who lives only for you.
    (DRAMATIC IRONY in
    that he does this, in
    effect)
10 suicide would put him in
    hell
11 by killing yourself
12 money lender, who has
    riches in abundance, and
    misuses them
13 decorate
14 a waxwork figure, a
    puppet (IRONY. The
    nurse refers to Paris as
    "a man of wax" Act 1,
    Scene 3, line 79)
15 if you lose your bravery
16 if you kill
17 misdirected
18 i.e. as a man and a
    husband
19 GUNPOWDER IMAGE
    recurs
20 blown apart by what
    should have protected
    you viz your intelligence
21 recently wishing to be
    dead

A pack of blessings lights upon thy back;
Happiness courts thee in her best array;
But, like a misbehav'd and *(1)* sullen wench,
Thou *(2)* pout'st upon thy fortune and thy love: –
Take heed, take heed, for such die miserable.   150
Go, get thee to thy love, as was *(3)* decreed,
Ascend her chamber, hence and comfort her:
But, look, thou stay not till *(4)* the watch be set,
For then thou canst not pass to Mantua;
Where thou shalt live till we can find a time   155
To *(5)* blaze your marriage, *(6)* reconcile your friends,
Beg pardon of the prince, and call thee back
With twenty hundred thousand times more joy
Than thou went'st forth in *(7)* lamentation. –
Go before, nurse: commend me to thy lady;   160
And bid her hasten all the house to bed,
Which heavy sorrow makes them *(8)* apt unto:
Romeo is coming.
NURSE O Lord, I could have stay'd here all the night
To hear good counsel: O, what learning is! –   165
My lord, I'll tell my lady you will come.
ROMEO Do so, and bid my sweet prepare to chide.
NURSE Here, sir, a ring she bid me give you sir:
Hie you, make haste, for it grows very late.   *(Exit.*
ROMEO How well my *(9)* comfort is reviv'd by this!   170
FRIAR LAWRENCE Go hence; good-night; and here stands *(10)* all your state:
Either be gone before the watch be set,
Or by the break of day disguis'd from hence:
(11) Sojourn in Mantua; I'll find out your man,
And he shall signify from time to time   175
Every good *(12)* hap to you that chances here:
Give me thy hand; 'tis late: farewell; good-night
ROMEO But that a *(13)* joy past joy calls out to me,
It were a grief so *(14)* brief to part with thee:
Farewell.   *(Exeunt.*   180

1	sulky girl
2	pulls faces at (He has reason to in fact, his fortune is not propitious)
3	planned
4	the guard is posted at the gates
5	publish
6	bring together, in friendship, supporters of both sides, through the marriage
7	crying sorrowfully
8	ready to do
9	happiness
10	everything depends on your following instructions
11	stay for a time
12	happening (DRAMATIC IRONY that false reports are sent to Mantua)
13	indescribable (joy)
14	to part with you so quickly

ACT THREE, SCENE FOUR
A ROOM IN CAPULET'S HOUSE.

Enter CAPULET, LADY CAPULET *and* PARIS.

CAPULET Things have ⁽¹⁾ fallen out, sir, so unluckily
  That we have had no time to ⁽²⁾ move our daughter:
  Look you, she lov'd her kinsman Tybalt dearly,
  And so did I; well, we were born to die.
  'Tis very late, she'll not come down to-night: 5
  I ⁽³⁾ promise you, but for your company,
  I would have been a-bed an hour ago.
PARIS These times of ⁽⁴⁾ woe afford no time to woo. –
  Madam, good-night: commend me to your daughter.
LADY CAPULET I will, and know her mind early to-morrow; 10
  To-night she's ⁽⁵⁾ mew'd up to her heaviness.
CAPULET ⁽⁶⁾ Sir Paris, I will make a ⁽⁷⁾ desperate tender
  Of my child's love: I think she will be rul'd
  In all respects by me; nay, more, I doubt it not. –
  Wife, go you to her ere you go to bed; 15
  Acquaint her here of my ⁽⁸⁾ son Paris' love;
  And bid her, mark you me, on Wednesday next, –
  But, ⁽⁹⁾ soft! what day is this?
PARIS   Monday, my lord.
CAPULET Monday! ha, ha! Well, ⁽¹⁰⁾ Wednesday is too soon, 20
  O' Thursday let it be; – o' Thursday, tell her,
  She shall be married to this noble earl. –
  Will you be ready? do you like this haste?
  We'll keep no great ado, – ⁽¹¹⁾ a friend or two;
  For, hark you, Tybalt being slain so ⁽¹²⁾ late, 25
  It may be thought we held him ⁽¹³⁾ carelessly,
  Being our kinsman, if we revel much:
  Therefore we'll have some half a dozen friends,
  And ⁽¹⁴⁾ there an end. But what say you to Thursday?
PARIS My lord, I would that Thursday were to-morrow. 30
CAPULET Well, get you gone: o' Thursday be it then. –
  Go you to Juliet ere you go to bed,
  Prepare her, wife, ⁽¹⁵⁾ against this wedding-day. –
  Farewell, my lord. – Light to my chamber, ho!–
  Afore me, it is so very very late 35
  That we may call it early by and by. –
  Good-night.   *(Exeunt.*

1	happened
2	persuade
3	assure
4	misery
5	caged (as for hawks)
	DRAMATIC IRONY - as
	Capulet is arranging the
	marriage to Paris she is
	consummating her
	marriage to Romeo
6	The marriage to Paris is
	to be confirmed.
	(CHANCE has made
	Capulet forget his earlier
	advice to wait 2 years)
7	bold offer. (As a PARENT
	Capulet is certain that he
	is right in making this
	decision and that his
	CHILD will obey him.
	IRONY in that he is
	totally wrong.)
8	future son-in-law
9	wait
10	DRAMATIC IRONY - he
	does make it Wednesday
11	it will be a quiet wedding
	(IRONIC because it turns
	into a large crowd)
12	recently
13	did not care for him
	enough to mourn properly
14	that will be the limit
15	ready for (Lady Capulet is
	to give her daughter the
	news)

ACT THREE, SCENE FIVE
AN OPEN GALLERY TO JULIET'S CHAMBER, OVERLOOKING THE GARDEN.

Enter ROMEO *and* JULIET.

JULIET Wilt thou be gone? it is not yet near day:
It was the nightingale, and not the lark,
That pierc'd the *(1)* fearful hollow of thine ear;
Nightly she sings on yon pomegranate tree:
Believe me, love, it was the nightingale.   5

ROMEO It was the lark, the herald of the morn,
No nightingale: look, love, what *(2)* envious streaks
Do lace the *(3)* severing clouds in yonder east:
(4) Night's candles are burnt out, and *(5)* jocund day
Stands tiptoe on the misty mountain tops.   10
I must be gone and live, or stay and die.

JULIET Yon light is not daylight, I know it, I:
It is some *(6)* meteor that the sun exhales,
To be to thee this night a torch-bearer,
And light thee on thy way to Mantua: 15
Therefore stay yet, thou need'st not to be gone.

ROMEO Let me be ta'en, let me be put to death;
I am content, so thou wilt have it so.
I'll say yon gray is not the morning's eye,
'Tis but the pale *(7)* reflex of *(8)* Cynthia's brow;   20
Nor that is not the lark whose notes do beat
The *(9)* vaulty heaven so high above our heads:
I have more *(10)* care to stay than will to go.–
(11) Come, death, and welcome! Juliet wills it so. –
How is't, my soul? let's talk, – it is not day.   25

JULIET It is, it is, – hie hence, be gone, away!
It is the lark that sings so out of tune,
Straining harsh discords and unpleasing *(12)* sharps.
Some say the lark makes sweet *(13)* division;
This doth not so, for she divideth us: 30
Some say the lark and loathed toad *(14)* change eyes
O, now I would they had chang'd voices too!
Since *(15)* arm from arm that voice doth us *(16)* affray,
(17) Hunting thee hence with hunt's-up to the day.
O, now be gone; more light and light it grows.   35

ROMEO More light and light, – more dark and dark our woes!

1 full of fear, listening for sounds
2 malicious
3 the clouds are being parted by light
4 the stars
5 happy
6 Believed to be vapours drawn upwards from the earth and set on fire by the sun.
7 reflection
8 a name for the moon
9 arched
10 desire
11 DRAMATIC IRONY - he is joking, but death is waiting for him
12 shrill, off-key sounds
13 a run of musical notes
14 exchange
15 from each other's arms
16 startle
17 he is to be hunted out at daybreak
   PUN hunting song, "Hunt's Up" (presumably sung by the bird)

Enter Nurse.

NURSE Madam!

JULIET Nurse?

NURSE Your lady mother is coming to your chamber:
The day is broke; be wary, look about.   *(Exit.*   40

JULIET Then, window, let day in and let life out.

ROMEO Farewell, farewell! one kiss, and I'll descend.   *(Descends.*

JULIET Art thou gone so? my lord, my love, my friend!
(1) I must hear from thee every day i' the hour,
For in a minute there are many days: 45
O, by this (2) count I shall be much in years
Ere I again behold my Romeo!

ROMEO Farewell!
I will omit no opportunity
That may convey my greetings, love, to thee.   50

JULIET O, think'st thou we shall ever meet again?

ROMEO (3) I doubt it not; and all these woes shall serve
For sweet (4) discourses in our time to come.

JULIET O God! I have an (5) ill-divining soul!
Methinks I see thee, now thou art below,   55
As one dead in the bottom of a tomb:
Either my eyesight fails or thou (6) look'st pale.

ROMEO And trust me, love, in my eye so do you:
(7) Dry sorrow drinks our blood. Adieu, adieu!   *(Exit below.*

JULIET O fortune, fortune! all men call thee (8) fickle: 60
If thou art fickle, what dost thou with him
That is renown'd for faith? Be fickle, fortune;
For then, I hope, thou wilt not keep him long,
But send him back.

LADY CAPULET *(Within.)* Ho, daughter! are you up?   65

JULIET Who is't that calls? is it my lady mother?
Is she not (9) down so late, or up so early?
What unaccustom'd cause (10) procures her hither?

Enter LADY CAPULET.

LADY CAPULET Why, how now, Juliet!

JULIET   Madam, I am not well.   70

LADY CAPULET (11) Evermore weeping for your cousin's death?
What, wilt thou wash him from his grave with tears?
An if thou couldst, thou couldst not make him live;
Therefore have done: (12) some grief shows much of love
But much of grief shows still some want of (13) wit.   75

---

1 DRAMATIC IRONY - she knows nothing of the arrangement with Paris, which will preclude her from writing or receiving letters

2 account/addition

3 DRAMATIC IRONY - this is their last meeting when they are both alive

4 conversations

5 having PREMONITIONS of ill-fortune

6 DRAMATIC IRONY - this is exactly how they shall see each other next,

7 it was believed that sighing thinned the blood

8 changeable

9 i.e. gone to bed late

10 brings

11 DRAMATIC IRONY - Juliet is weeping at parting from Romeo

12 a moderate amount

13 always shows lack of good sense. (Lady Capulet is rather sharp with her daughter here, she is not sympathetic)

JULIET Yet let me weep for such a (1) feeling loss.

LADY CAPULET So shall you feel the loss, but not the friend
    Which you weep for.

JULIET   Feeling so the loss,
    I cannot choose but ever weep the (2) friend.   80

LADY CAPULET Well, girl, thou weep'st not so much for his death
    As that the villain lives which slaughter'd him.

JULIET What villain, madam?

LADY CAPULET   That same villain, Romeo.

JULIET Villain and he be many miles (3) asunder.   85
    God pardon him! I do, with all my heart;
    And yet no man (4) like he doth grieve my heart.

LADY CAPULET That is because the traitor murderer lives.

JULIET Ay, madam, (5) from the reach of these my hands.
    Would none but I might venge my cousin's death!   90

LADY CAPULET We will have vengeance for it, fear thou not:
    Then weep no more. I'll send to one in Mantua, –
    Where that same banish'd (6) runagate doth live, –
    Shall give him such an unaccustom'd (7) dram
    That he shall soon keep Tybalt company: 95
    And then I hope thou wilt be satisfied.

JULIET Indeed I never shall be satisfied
    With Romeo till I behold him – (8) dead, –
    Is my poor heart so for a kinsman vex'd:
    Madam, if you could find out but a man   100
    To bear a poison, I would (9) temper it,
    That Romeo should, upon receipt thereof,
    (10) Soon sleep in quiet. O, how my heart abhors
    To hear him nam'd – and cannot come to him, –
    To wreak the love I bore my cousin Tybalt   105
    Upon his body (11) that hath slaughter'd him!

LADY CAPULET Find thou the (12) means, and I'll find such a man.
    But now I'll tell thee (13) joyful tidings, girl.

JULIET And joy comes well in such a needy time:
    What are they, (14) I beseech your ladyship?   110

LADY CAPULET Well, well, thou hast a (15) careful father, child;
    One who, to put thee from thy (16) heaviness,
    Hath (17) sorted out a sudden day of joy
    That thou expect'st not, nor I look'd not for.

JULIET Madam, (18) in happy time, what day is that?   115

LADY CAPULET Marry, my child, early next Thursday morn
    The gallant, young, and noble gentleman,

---

1   deeply felt. (She is referring to Romeo)

2   i.e. Romeo

3   apart

4   as much as

5   she wants to hold Romeo close to her

6   vagabond

7   measure of poison (the IRONY is that he will do this himself)

8   she means that her heart is dead (the IRONY is that he will be dead when she next sees him)

9   mix

10   she would give him a draught to bring him sweet dreams, not to poison him

11   the body of the man i.e. Romeo

12   of such a poison

13   these are the last "tidings" she wants to hear

14   (N.B. the formality with which she addresses her mother)

15   one who cares

16   sadness

17   arranged an unanticipated pleasure

18   how appropriate at this moment

The (1) County Paris, at St. Peter's Church,
Shall happily make thee there a joyful bride.
JULIET Now, by St. Peter's Church, and Peter too,   120
(2) He shall not make me there a joyful bride.
I wonder at this haste; that I must wed
(3) Ere he that should be husband comes to woo.
I pray you, tell my lord and father, madam,
I will not marry yet; and when I do, I swear   125
It shall be Romeo, whom you know I hate,
Rather than Paris: – these are news indeed!
LADY CAPULET Here comes your father; (4) tell him so yourself,
And see how he will take it (5) at your hands.

Enter CAPULET *and* Nurse.

CAPULET When the sun sets, the air doth (6) drizzle dew;   130
But for the sunset of my brother's son
It rains downright. –
How now! a (7) conduit, girl? what, still in tears?
Evermore showering? In one little body
Thou (8) counterfeit'st a bark, a sea, a wind: 135
For still thy eyes, which I may call the sea,
Do ebb and flow with tears; the (9) bark thy body is,
Sailing in this salt flood; the winds thy sighs;
Who, – raging with thy tears, and they with them, –
(10) Without a sudden calm, will (11) overset   140
Thy tempest-tossed body. – How now, wife!
Have you deliver'd to her our (12) decree?
LADY CAPULET Ay, sir; but she will none, she gives you thanks.
(13) I would the fool were married to her grave!
CAPULET Soft! (14) take me with you, take me with you wife.   145
How! will she none? doth she not give us thanks?
Is she not (15) proud? doth she not count her bless'd
Unworthy as she is, that we have wrought
So worthy a gentleman to be her bridegroom?
JULIET Not proud you (16) have; but thankful that you have: 150
Proud can I never be of what I (17) hate;
But thankful even for hate that (18) is meant love.
CAPULET How now, how now, (19) chop-logic! What is this?
Proud, – and, I thank you, – and, I thank you not; –
And yet not proud: – mistress (20) minion, you,   155
Thank me no thankings, nor proud me no prouds,
But (21) fettle your fine joints 'gainst Thursday next,

1   this marriage is now more expedient than ever in the opinion of Capulet

2   this is the first instance of Juliet's disobedience to her parents

3   he has hardly paid court to her

4   Lady Capulet does not want to face her husband with this news

5   from you

6   he is referring to Juliet's tears

7   a fountain of tears

8   you are like a ship in a storm (IRONY cf. Romeo's "seasick, weary bark", Act 5, Scene 3 line 119)

9   ship

10   unless

11   overturn, capsize

12   command (as a father his word was as law)

13   IRONY in that she will be. The idea of DEATH as JULIET'S LOVER recurs. (N.B. Lady Capulet is very harsh towards her disobedient daughter)

14   explain to me

15   i.e. of her father's care for her

16   i.e. arranged it

17   not Paris, but becoming his wife

18   when you intended me to love it

19   quibbling words

20   low thing (Capulet is violently angry at her disobedience)

21   make yourself ready (by dressing for a wedding)

To go with Paris to St. Peter's Church,
Or I will drag thee on a *(1)* hurdle thither.
Out, you *(2)* green-sickness carrion! out, *(3)* you baggage!   160
You *(4)* tallow-face!

LADY CAPULET   Fie, fie! *(5)* what, are you mad?

JULIET Good father, I beseech you on my knees,
Hear me with patience but to speak a word.

CAPULET Hang thee, young baggage! disobedient wretch!   165
I tell thee what, – get thee to church o' Thursday,
Or never after look me in the face:
Speak not, reply not, do not answer me;
My fingers *(6)* itch. – Wife, we scarce thought us bless'd
That God had *(7)* lent us but this only child;   170
But now I see this one is one too much,
And that we have a curse in having her:
Out on her, *(8)* hilding!

NURSE   God in heaven bless her! –
You are to blame, my lord, to *(9)* rate her so.   175

CAPULET And why, *(10)* my lady wisdom? hold your tongue,
Good prudence; *(11)* smatter with your gossips, go.

NURSE I speak *(12)* no treason.

CAPULET   O, *(13)* God ye good-den!

NURSE May not one speak?   180

CAPULET   Peace, you mumbling fool!
Utter your *(14)* gravity o'er gossip's bowl,
For here we need it not.

LADY CAPULET   You are too *(15)* hot.

CAPULET *(16)* God's bread! it makes me mad: 185
Day, night, hour, *(17)* tide, time, work, play,
Alone, in company, still my care hath been
To have her match'd, and having now provided
A gentleman of noble parentage,
Of *(18)* fair demesnes, youthful, and nobly *(19)* train'd,   190
Stuff'd, as they say, with honourable *(20)* parts,
(21) Proportion'd as one's heart could wish a man, –
And then to have a wretched *(22)* puling fool,
A whining *(23)* mammet, in her fortune's *(24)* tender,
To answer, *I'll not wed, – I cannot love,*   195
(25) I am too young, – I pray you pardon me; –
But, an you will not wed, *(26)* I'll pardon you:
(27) Graze where you will, you shall not house with me:
Look to't, think on't, *(28)* I do not use to jest.

1	a frame for dragging prisoners through the streets
2	pale-faced corpse
3	hussy
4	sallow faced creature
5	even Lady Capulet is alarmed that her husband could be so extreme
6	i.e. to hit her for defying him
7	given (DRAMATIC IRONY - he will not see her alive again)
8	hussy
9	abuse, berate
10	Capulet is being sardonic. He means the opposite.
11	prattle
12	nothing against you
13	God give you good evening i.e. go
14	serious thoughts, but he is being sardonic
15	extreme in your anger
16	the communion host
17	season
18	estates
19	educated
20	qualities
21	a reference to his good looks
22	whimpering
23	puppet
24	offer of good fortune
25	IRONY - he had said this himself
26	send you packing
27	feed
28	it is not in my nature to

Thursday is near; lay hand on heart, *(1)* advise: 200   *1* be advised
An you be mine, I'll give you to my friend;
An you be not, hang, beg, starve, die i' the streets,
For, by my soul, I'll ne'er acknowledge thee,
Nor what is mine shall *(2)* never do thee good: *2* you forfeit your
Trust to't, bethink you, I'll *(3)* not be forsworn.   *(Exit.* 205   inheritance

JULIET Is there no pity sitting in the clouds,   *3* not break my word,
That sees into the bottom of my grief?   neither my threats to you
O, sweet my mother, cast me not away!   nor my promise to Paris
Delay this marriage for a month, a week;
Or, if you do not, make the bridal bed   210
In that dim monument where Tybalt lies.

LADY CAPULET *(4)* Talk not to me, for I'll not speak a word;   *4* Lady Capulet is cruelly
Do as thou wilt, for I have done with thee.   *(Exit.*   hostile to Juliet here and

JULIET O God! – O nurse! how shall this be prevented?   contributes, with the
My husband is on *(5)* earth, my *(6)* faith in heaven;   215   nurse's betrayal, to her
How shall that faith return again to earth,   terrible isolation
Unless that husband send it me from heaven   *5* alive
(7) By leaving earth? – comfort me, counsel me. –   *6* marriage, recorded in
Alack, alack, that heaven should *(8)* practise stratagems   heaven
Upon so soft a subject as myself! –   220   *7* by dying
What say'st thou? hast thou not a word of joy?   *8* plot against me
Some comfort, nurse.

NURSE   Faith, here 'tis: Romeo
Is banished; and *(9)* all the world to nothing   *9* I bet you the whole world
That he dares ne'er come back to *(10)* challenge you;   225 *10* claim you as his wife
Or, if he do, it needs must be by stealth.
Then, since the case so stands as now it doth,
I think it best you married with the county.
O, he's a lovely gentleman!
Romeo's a *(11)* dishclout to him; an eagle, madam,   230 *11* dishcloth
Hath not so *(12)* green, so quick, so fair an eye   *12* he has green eyes
As Paris hath. *(13)* Beshrew my very heart,   *13* curse
I think you are happy in this second *(14)* match,   *14* marriage
For it excels your first: or if it did not,
Your first is dead; or 'twere as good he were,   235
As *(15)* living here, and you no use of him.   *15* you living here and not

JULIET Speakest thou from thy heart?   able to use him as your

NURSE From my soul too,   husband
Or else beshrew them both.

JULIET *(16)* Amen!   240 *16* i.e. that your heart

NURSE What?   should be cursed

JULIET Well, (1) thou hast comforted me marvellous much.
    Go in; and tell my lady I am gone,
    (2) Having displeas'd my father, to Lawrence' cell
    To make confession, and to be absolv'd.   245
NURSE Marry, I will; and this is wisely done.   *(Exit.*
JULIET (3) Ancient damnation! O most wicked fiend!
    Is it more sin to wish me thus forsworn,
    Or to (4) dispraise my lord with that same tongue
    Which she hath prais'd him with (5) above compare   250
    So many thousand times? – Go, (6) counsellor;
    Thou and my (7) bosom henceforth shall be (8) twain. –
    I'll to the friar, to know his remedy;
    If all else fail, (9) myself have power to die.   *(Exit.*

1	IRONY - she means the opposite
2	she really intends to seek help from Friar Lawrence
3	old wicked devil
4	speak against
5	above comparison
6	confidante (ironical because she is no longer)
7	you and my secrets
8	are separated for ever
9	I will kill myself

ACT FOUR, SCENE ONE
FRIAR LAWRENCE'S CELL.

Enter FRIAR LAWRENCE *and* PARIS.

FRIAR LAWRENCE On Thursday, sir? the time is very short.
PARIS My (10) father Capulet will have it so;
    And I am (11) nothing slow to slack his haste.
FRIAR LAWRENCE You say you do not know the lady's mind:
    (12) Uneven is the course, I like it not.   5
PARIS Immoderately she weeps for Tybalt's death,
    And therefore have I little talk'd of love;
    For Venus smiles not in a house of tears.
    Now, sir, her father counts it dangerous
    That she doth give her sorrow so much (13) sway;   10
    And, in his wisdom, (14) hastes our marriage,
    To stop the (15) inundation of her tears;
    Which, too (16) much minded by herself alone,
    May be put from her (17) by society:
    Now do you know the reason of this haste.   15
FRIAR LAWRENCE *(Aside.)* I would I knew not why it should be slow'd. –
    Look, sir, here comes the lady towards my cell.

    Enter JULIET.
PARIS Happily met, my lady and my wife!

10	future father-in-law
11	not encouraging him to wait
12	irregular, not normal circumstances (because the house is in mourning)
13	influence (Capulet has not given much thought to his verbal violence towards her!)
14	hastens
15	pouring
16	gives way to them when she is alone
17	i.e. companionship (may take her mind off her grief)

JULIET [1] That may be, sir, when I may be a wife.

PARIS That may be must be, love, on Thursday next.   20

JULIET What must be shall be.

FRIAR LAWRENCE   That's a certain text.

PARIS Come you to make confession to this father?

JULIET To answer that, I should confess to you.

PARIS Do not deny to him that you love me.   25

JULIET I will confess to you that I love him.

PARIS So will ye, I am sure, that you love me.

JULIET If I do so, it will be of more [2] price

    Being spoke behind your back than to your face.

PARIS Poor soul, thy face is much abus'd with tears.   30

JULIET The tears have got small victory by that;

    For it was bad enough before their [3] spite.

PARIS Thou wrong'st it more than tears with that report.

JULIET That is no slander, sir, which is a truth;

    And what I spake I [4] spake it to my face.   35

PARIS Thy face is mine, and thou hast slander'd it.

JULIET It may be so, for it is [5] not mine own. –

    Are you at leisure, holy father, now;

    Or shall I come to you at evening mass?

FRIAR LAWRENCE [6] My leisure serves me, pensive daughter, now. –   40

    My lord, we must [7] entreat the time alone.

PARIS God [8] shield I should disturb devotion! –

    Juliet, on Thursday early will I rouse you:

    Till then, adieu; and keep this holy kiss.   *(Exit.*

JULIET O, shut the door! and when thou has done so,   45

    Come weep with me; past hope, past cure, past help!

FRIAR LAWRENCE Ah, Juliet, I already know thy grief;

    It strains me past the [9] compass of my wits:

    I hear thou must, and nothing may [10] prorogue it,

    On Thursday next be married to this county.   50

JULIET Tell me not, friar, that thou hear'st of this,

    Unless thou tell me how I may prevent it:

    If, in thy wisdom, thou canst give no help,

    Do thou but call my resolution wise,

    And with this [11] knife I'll help it presently.   55

    God join'd my heart and Romeo's, thou our hands;

    And [12] ere this hand, by thee to Romeo seal'd,

    Shall be the [13] label to another deed,

    Or my true heart with treacherous revolt

    Turn to another, [14] this shall slay them [15] both: 60

---

1 Both of them indulge in word play and PUNNING here

2 value

3 the damage done by tears

4 openly

5 IRONY - it belongs to Romeo

6 I am free now

7 I beg you to leave us alone

8 forbid

9 it is beyond my ability

10 postpone

11 she will immediately kill herself

12 before

13 the seal to another contract (in law)

14 i.e. the knife

15 hand and heart

Therefore, out of thy _(1)_ long-experienc'd time,
Give me some _(2)_ present counsel; or, behold,
'Twixt my _(3)_ extremes and me this bloody knife
Shall play the _(4)_ umpire; _(5)_ arbitrating that
Which the _(6)_ commission of thy years and _(7)_ art   65
_(8)_ Could to no issue of true honour bring.
Be not so long to speak; I long to die,
If what thou speak'st speak _(9)_ not of remedy.

FRIAR LAWRENCE _(10)_ Hold, daughter: I do spy a kind of hope,
Which _(11)_ craves as desperate _(12)_ an execution   70
As that is desperate which we would prevent.
If, rather than to marry County Paris,
Thou hast the strength of will to slay thyself,
Then is it likely thou wilt undertake
A thing like death to _(13)_ chide away this shame,   75
That cop'st with death himself to _(14)_ scape from it;
And, if thou dar'st, I'll give thee remedy.

JULIET O, bid me leap, rather than marry Paris,
From off the battlements of yonder tower;
Or walk in _(15)_ thievish ways; or bid me lurk   80
Where serpents are; chain me with roaring bears;
Or shut me nightly in a _(16)_ charnel-house,
O'er-cover'd quite with dead men's rattling bones,
With _(17)_ reeky shanks, and yellow _(18)_ chapless skulls;
Or bid me go into a new-made grave,   85
And hide me with a dead man in his shroud;
Things that, to hear them told, have made me tremble
And I will do it without fear or doubt,
To live an _(19)_ unstain'd wife to my sweet love.

FRIAR LAWRENCE Hold, then; go home, be merry, give consent   90
To marry Paris; Wednesday is to-morrow;
To-morrow night look that thou lie alone,
Let not thy nurse lie with thee in thy chamber:
Take thou this _(20)_ vial, being then in bed,
And this _(21)_ distilled liquor drink thou off: 95
When, _(22)_ presently, through all thy veins shall run
A cold and drowsy _(23)_ humour; for no pulse
Shall keep his _(24)_ native progress, but surcease:
No warmth, no breath, shall testify thou liv'st;
The rose in thy lips and cheeks shall fade   100
To _(25)_ paly ashes; thy eyes' windows fall,
Like death, when he shuts up the day of life;

1 wisdom of age
2 instant advice
3 extremes of distress
4 play the judge
5 deciding
6 authority
7 skill
8 the usual legal process cannot settle the issue
9 if you cannot find a solution
10 wait
11 demands
12 carrying out
13 banish this disgrace
14 i.e. the bigamous marriage to Paris
15 lanes frequented by robbers
16 place were bones were kept which were dug up when preparing new graves
17 foul smelling
18 no lower jaw bone
19 unmarked by adultery
20 small bottle
21 i.e. which will run thro' the whole body
22 immediately
23 liquid
24 natural progress, but cease
25 pale, wan

Each part, depriv'd of *(1)* supple government,
Shall, stiff and stark and cold, appear like death:
And in this borrow'd likeness of *(2)* shrunk death   **105**
Thou shalt continue two-and-forty hours,
And then awake as from a pleasant sleep.
Now, when the bridegroom in the morning comes
To rouse thee from thy bed, there art thou dead
Then, – as the manner of our country, is, –   **110**
In thy best robes, *(3)* uncover'd, on the bier,
Thou shalt be borne to that same ancient vault
Where all the kindred of the Capulets lie.
In the meantime, *(4)* against thou shalt awake,
Shall Romeo by my letters know our *(5)* drift;   **115**
And hither shall he come: and he and I
Will *(6)* watch thy waking, and that very night
Shall Romeo bear thee hence to Mantua.
And this shall free thee from this present shame
If *(7)* no inconstant toy nor womanish fear   **120**
(8) Abate thy valour in the acting it.
JULIET Give me, give me! O, tell not me of fear!
FRIAR LAWRENCE Hold; get you gone, be strong and *(9)* prosperous
In this resolve: I'll send a friar with speed
To Mantua, with my letters to thy lord.   **125**
JULIET <u>Love give me strength!</u> and strength *(10)* shall help afford.
Farewell, dear father!   *(Exeunt.*

ACT FOUR, SCENE TWO
HALL IN CAPULET'S HOUSE.

Enter CAPULET, LADY CAPULET, Nurse, *and* Servants.

CAPULET So many guests invite as here are writ.
    (Exit first Servant.
Sirrah, *(11)* go hire me twenty *(12)* cunning cooks.
2 SERVANT You shall have *(13)* none ill, sir; for I'll try if they can *(14)* lick
their fingers.
CAPULET How canst thou try them so?   **5**
2 SERVANT Marry, sir, 'tis an ill cook that cannot lick his own fingers:
therefore he that cannot lick his fingers goes not with me.
CAPULET Go, be gone. –   *(Exit second* Servant.
We shall be much *(15)* unfurnish'd for this time, –

---

1 control of movement

2 shrivelled

3 face uncovered in the coffin

4 in readiness for when . . .

5 plan

6 wait for

7 lack of resolution (because of fear)

8 takes away your bravery

9 successful

10 i.e. the strength of her <u>love</u>

11 DRAMATIC IRONY -
1. the half dozen friends of Capulet's original plan has obviously been extended.
2. the panic & rush of the feast will be in vain.

12 expert

13 no bad ones

14 proverb (the cook must taste his dishes!)

15 unprepared

What, is my daughter gone to Friar Lawrence?   **10**

NURSE Ay, *(1)* forsooth.

CAPULET Well, he may chance to do some good on her:

     (2) A peevish self-will'd harlotry it is.

NURSE See where she comes from *(3)* shrift with merry look.

Enter JULIET.

CAPULET How now, my headstrong! where have you been *(4)* gadding?   **15**

JULIET Where I have learn'd me to *(5)* repent the sin

     Of disobedient opposition

     To you and your *(6)* behests; and am *(7)* enjoin'd

     By holy Lawrence to fall prostrate here,

     And beg your pardon: – pardon, I beseech you!   **20**

     Henceforward I am ever rul'd by you.

CAPULET Send for the *(8)* county; go tell him of this:

     I'll have this *(9)* knot knit up *(10)* to-morrow morning.

JULIET I met the youthful lord at Lawrence cell;

     And gave him what *(11)* becomed love I might,   **25**

     Not stepping o'er the bounds of modesty.

CAPULET Why, I am glad on't; this is well, – stand up, –

     (12) This is as't should be. – Let me see the county;

     Ay, marry, go, I say, and fetch him hither. –

     Now, afore God, this reverend holy friar,   **30**

     All our whole city is much *(13)* bound to him.

JULIET Nurse, will you go with me into my *(14)* closet,

     To help me sort such needful *(15)* ornaments

     As you think fit to furnish me to-morrow?

LADY CAPULET No, not till Thursday; there is time enough.   **35**

CAPULET Go, nurse, go with her. – *(16)* We'll to church to-morrow.

                 (Exeunt JULIET *and* Nurse.

LADY CAPULET We shall be short in our provision:

     'Tis now near night.

CAPULET   Tush, I will *(17)* stir about,

     And all things shall be well I *(18)* warrant thee, wife: **40**

     Go thou to Juliet, help to *(19)* deck her;

     I'll not to bed to-night; – let me alone;

     I'll play the housewife for this once. – *(20)* What, ho! –

     They are all forth: well, I will walk myself

     To County Paris, to prepare him up   **45**

     Against to-morrow: my heart is wondrous light

     Since this same wayward girl is so *(21)* reclaim'd.

                           (Exeunt.

Notes

1   certainly

2   sullen, obstinate hussy

3   confession

4   wandering off to

5   IRONY Juliet is playing the part of dutiful daughter

6   commands

7   advised

8   County Paris

9   marriage

10   This must be Wednesday. Fate has intervened again, Capulet is so taken with Juliet's reversal that he advances the wedding, so throwing all Friar Lawrence's plans into disarray.

11   proper

12   that she is obeying her father

13   in debt

14   room

15   decoration, not only of clothing, but of jewellery

16   he insists on advancing the day

17   be busy with the arrangements

18   promise

19   prepare her dress

20   he shouts to the servants; they are already off to see to the arrangements

21   IRONICALLY he thinks that she is now obedient

ACT FOUR, SCENE THREE
JULIET'S CHAMBER.

Enter JULIET *and* Nurse.

JULIET Ay, those attires are best: – but, gentle nurse,
I pray thee, leave me to myself to-night;
For I have need of many *(1)* orisons
To move the heavens to smile upon my *(2)* state,
Which, well thou know'st, is *(3)* cross and full of sin.   5

Enter LADY CAPULET.
LADY CAPULET What, are you busy, ho? *(4)* need you my help?
JULIET No, madam; we have *(5)* cull'd such necessaries
As are *(6)* behoveful for our state to-morrow:
So please you, let me now be left alone,
And let the nurse this night sit up with you;   10
For I am sure you have your hands full all
In this so sudden business.
LADY CAPULET   Good-night:
Get thee to bed, and rest; for thou hast need.
                    (Exeunt LADY CAPULET *and* Nurse.
JULIET Farewell! – God knows when we shall meet again.   15
I have a faint cold fear *(7)* thrills through my veins,
That almost freezes up the *(8)* heat of life:
I'll call them back again to comfort me; –
Nurse! – What should she do here?
My dismal scene I needs must act alone. –   20
Come, *(9)* vial. –
What if this mixture do not work at all?
Shall I be married, then, to-morrow morning? –
No, no; *(10)* this shall forbid it: – lie thou there. –
                    (Laying down her dagger.
What if it be a poison, which the friar   25
Subtly hath *(11)* minister'd to have me dead,
Lest in this marriage he should be dishonour'd,
Because he married me before to Romeo?
I fear it is: and yet methinks it should not,
For he hath still been *(12)* tried a holy man: –   30
I will not entertain so bad a thought. –
How if, when I am laid into the tomb,
I wake before the time that Romeo

1	prayers
2	situation
3	perverse (bigamous)
4	Lady Capulet is now being motherly
5	decided upon
6	fitting
7	shivers
8	her blood
9	bottle
10	the knife
11	given to me
12	proved by the test of experience

Come to (1) redeem me? there's a fearful point!   *1   rescue*
Shall I not then be stifled in the vault,   **40**
To whose foul mouth no (2) healthsome air breathes in,   *2   wholesome*
And there die (3) strangled ere my Romeo comes?   *3   suffocated*
Or, if I live, is it not very like
The horrible (4) conceit of death and night,   *4   imaginings*
Together with the terror of the place, –   **45**
As in a vault, an ancient (5) receptacle,   *5   sepulchre*
Where, for these many hundred years, the bones
Of all my buried ancestors are pack'd;
Where bloody Tybalt, yet but (6) green in earth,   *6   freshly buried*
Lies festering in his shroud; where, as they say,   **50**
At some hours in the night spirits resort; –
Alack, alack, is it not like that I,
So early waking, – what with loathsome smells,
And shrieks like (7) mandrakes' torn out of the earth,   *7   a plant which shrieks*
That living mortals, hearing them, run mad; –   **55**   *when pulled from the*
O, if I wake, shall I not be (8) distraught,   *ground*
(9) Environed with all these hideous fears?   *8   driven mad*
And madly play with my forefathers' (10) joints?   *9   surrounded*
And pluck the (11) mangled Tybalt from his shroud?   *10   bones*
And, in this rage, with some great kinsman's bone,   **60**   *11   IRONY - Romeo uses the*
As with a club, dash out my desperate brains? –   *same word*
O, look! methinks I see my cousin's ghost
Seeking out Romeo, that did (12) spit his body   *12   run his sword right*
Upon a rapier's point: – (13) stay, Tybalt, stay! –   *through his body*
Romeo, I come! this do I drink to thee.   *13   stop*

(Throws herself on the bed.

ACT FOUR, SCENE FOUR
HALL IN CAPULET'S HOUSE.   *14   the room where pastry*
                                            was made

Enter LADY CAPULET *and* Nurse.   *15   morning bell*
                                            16   pies
LADY CAPULET Hold, take these keys, and fetch more spices, nurse.   *17   it is not certain who this*
NURSE They call for dates and quinces in the (14) pastry.   *is, but as he is talking to*
                                            the nurse it is probably
    Enter CAPULET.   *her first name. The*
CAPULET Come, stir, stir, stir! the second cock hath crow'd,   *possibility is*
    The (15) curfew bell hath rung, 'tis three o'clock: –   *corroborated by her over*
    Look to the (16) bak'd meats, good (17) Angelica: **5**   *familiarity in line 7*

71

Spare not for cost.

NURSE   Go, you *(1)* cot-quean, go,
Get you to bed; faith, you'll be sick to-morrow
For this night's watching.

CAPULET No, not a whit: what! I have *(2)* watch'd ere now   10
All night for lesser cause, and ne'er been sick.

LADY CAPULET Ay, you have been *(3)* a mouse-hunt in your time;
But I will watch you from such watching now.
                              (Exeunt LADY CAPULET *and* Nurse.

CAPULET A *(4)* jealous-hood, a jealous-hood – Now fellow,

Enter Servants, *with spits, logs, and baskets.*
What's there?   15

1 SERVANT Things for the cook, sir; but I know not what.

CAPULET Make haste, make haste.   *(Exit* 1 Servant.
                    – Sirrah, fetch drier logs:
Call Peter, he will show thee where they are.

2 SERVANT I have a head, sir, that will find out logs,   20
And never trouble Peter for the matter.   *(Exit.*

CAPULET Mass, and well said; a merry *(5)* whoreson, ha!
Thou shalt be *(6)* logger-head. – Good faith, 'tis day:
The county will be here with music *(7)* straight,
For so he said he would: – I hear him near.   *(Music within.* 25
Nurse! – wife! – what, ho! – what, nurse, I say!

Re-enter Nurse.
Go waken Juliet, go and *(8)* trim her up;
I'll go and chat with Paris: – hie, make haste,
Make haste; the bridegroom he is come already:
Make haste, I say.   *(Exeunt.* 30

ACT FOUR, SCENE FIVE
JULIET'S CHAMBER; JULIET ON THE BED.

Enter Nurse.

NURSE Mistress! – what, mistress! – Juliet! – *(9)* fast, I warrant her, she: –
Why, lamb! – why, lady! – fie, you slug-a-bed!–
Why, love, I say! – madam! sweetheart! – why, bride! –
What, not a word? – you take your *(10)* pennyworths now:
Sleep for a week; for the next night, I warrant,   5

---

1 to Capulet because he is
     interfering with woman's
     work

2 stayed awake

3 a womanizer (Lady
     Capulet rather snappily
     says that she will prevent
     all that from now on)

4 woman

5 rascal

6 a wooden head (PUN on
     logs) Capulet is now in a
     good humour as
     everything seems to be
     going according to his
     plans.

7 immediately

8 dress

9 fast asleep

10 all the sleep you can get
      now

The County Paris hath set up ⁽¹⁾ his rest

That you shalt ⁽²⁾ rest but little. – God forgive me,

Marry, and amen, how sound is she asleep!

I needs must wake her. – Madam, madam, madam. –

Ay, let the county ⁽³⁾ take you in your bed;

He'll fright you up, i' faith. – ⁽⁴⁾ Will it not be?

What, dress'd! and in your clothes! and ⁽⁵⁾ down again!

I must needs wake you: – lady! lady! lady! –

Alas, alas! – Help, help! my lady's dead! –

O, ⁽⁶⁾ well-a-day, that ever I was born! –

Some ⁽⁷⁾ aqua-vitæ, ho! – my lord! my lady!

Enter LADY CAPULET.

LADY CAPULET What noise is here?

NURSE   O ⁽⁸⁾ lamentable day!

LADY CAPULET What is the matter?

NURSE   Look, look! O heavy day!

LADY CAPULET O me, O me! – my child, my only life,

Revive, look up, or I will die with thee! –

Help, help! – call help.

Enter CAPULET.

CAPULET For shame bring Juliet forth; her lord is come.

NURSE She's dead, deceas'd, she's dead: alack the day!

LADY CAPULET Alack the day, she's dead, she's dead, she's dead!

CAPULET Ha! let me see her: – out, alas! she's cold;

Her blood is settled, and her joints are stiff;

Life and these lips have long been separated:

Death lies on her like an untimely frost

Upon the sweetest flower of all the field.

NURSE O lamentable day!

LADY CAPULET   O woeful time!

CAPULET Death, that hath ta'en her hence to make me wail,

Ties up my tongue, and will not let me speak.

Enter FRIAR LAWRENCE *and* PARIS, *with* Musicians.

FRIAR LAWRENCE ⁽⁹⁾ Come, is the bride ready to go to church?

CAPULET Ready to go, but never to return:–

O son, the night before thy wedding-day

Hath death lain with thy bride: – there she lies,

Flower as she was, ⁽¹⁰⁾ deflowered by him.

Death is my son-in-law, death is my heir;

1	put up all his money (as in a card game)
2	PUN on rest (and bawdy innuendo which she cannot resist.)
3	a further reference to love making
4	is that not so?
5	lain down
6	alas
7	reviving alcohol probably brandy
8	sorrowful
9	DRAMATIC IRONY he knows she is not!
10	lost her virginity to

Line numbers: 10, 15, 20, 25, 30, 35, 40

My daughter he hath wedded: I will die,

And leave him all; life, *(1)* living, *(2)* all is death's.

PARIS Have I thought long to see this morning's face,

And doth it give me such a sight as this?   45

LADY CAPULET Accurs'd, unhappy, wretched, hateful day!

Most miserable hour that e'er time saw

In *(3)* lasting labour of his pilgrimage!

But one, poor one, one poor and loving child,

But one thing to rejoice and *(4)* solace in,   50

And cruel death hath *(5)* catch'd it from my sight!

NURSE O woe! O woeful, woeful, woeful day!

Most lamentable day, most woeful day,

That ever, ever, I did yet behold!

O day! O day! O day! O hateful day!   55

Never was seen so black a day as this:

O woeful day, O woeful day!

PARIS *(6)* Beguil'd, divorced, wronged, spited, slain!

Most detestable death, by thee beguil'd,

By cruel cruel thee quite *(7)* overthrown! –   60

O love! O life! – not life, but love in death!

CAPULET Despis'd, distressed, hated, martyr'd, kill'd! –

(8) Uncomfortable time, why cam'st thou now

To murder, murder our *(9)* solemnity? –

O child! O child! – my soul, and not my child! –   65

Dead art thou, dead! – alack, my child is dead;

And with my child my joys are buried!

FRIAR LAWRENCE Peace, ho, for shame! *(10)* confusion's cure lives not

In these confusions. Heaven and yourself

Had part in this fair maid; now heaven hath all,   70

And all the better is it for the maid:

Your *(11)* part in her you could not keep from death;

But heaven keeps his *(12)* part in eternal life.

The most you sought was her *(13)* promotion;

For 'twas your heaven she should be *(14)* advanc'd: 75

And weep ye now, seeing she is *(15)* advanc'd

Above the clouds, as high as heaven itself?

O, in this love, you love your child so ill

That you run mad, seeing that she is *(16)* well:

She's not well married that lives married long;   80

But she's best married that dies married young.

Dry up your tears, and stick your *(17)* rosemary.

On this fair *(18)* corse; and as the custom is,

1	property
2	because she cannot now have children
3	endless toil
4	take comfort
5	snatched
6	deceived - Paris sees Death as an adulterer
7	I am quite overthrown
8	lacking any comfort
9	marriage feast
10	the remedy for disaster is not in these extremes of distress
11	i.e. her body IRONY because she is not dead
12	her soul
13	i.e. by the marriage to Paris
14	i.e. in status
15	raised
16	i.e. now in heaven
17	herb for remembrance
18	corpse

In all her best array bear her to church:

For though *(1)* fond nature bids us all lament,   85

Yet nature's tears are reason's *(2)* merriment.

CAPULET All things that we ordained *(3)* festival

Turn from their *(4)* office to black funeral:

Our *(5)* instruments to melancholy bells;

Our wedding cheer to a sad burial feast;   90

Our solemn hymns to sullen *(6)* dirges change;

Our bridal flowers serve for a buried corse,

And all things change them to the contrary.

FRIAR LAWRENCE Sir, go you in, – and, madam, go with him; –

And go, Sir Paris; – every one prepare   95

To follow this fair corse unto her grave:

The heavens do *(7)* lower upon you for some ill;

Move them no more by *(8)* crossing their high will.

                  (Exeunt CAPULET, LADY CAPULET, PARIS *and* Friar.

1 MUSICIAN Faith, we may *(9)* put up our pipes and be gone.

NURSE Honest good fellows, ah, put up, put up;   100

For, well you know, this a pitiful *(10)* case.

                            (Exit.

1 MUSICIAN Ay, by my troth, the *(11)* case may be amended.

   Enter PETER.

PETER Musicians, O, musicians, *(12)* Heart's ease, Heart's ease: O, an

you will have me live, play *Heart's ease.*

1 MUSICIAN Why *Heart's ease?*   105

PETER O, musicians, because my heart itself plays *(13)* My heart is full of

woe: O, play me some merry *(14)* dump to comfort me.

1 MUSICIAN Not a dump we; 'tis no time to play now.

PETER You will not, then?

1 MUSICIAN No.   110

PETER I will, then, give it you *(15)* soundly.

1 MUSICIAN What will you give us?

PETER No money, on my faith; but the *(16)* gleek,

– I will give you the minstrel.

1 MUSICIAN Then will I give you the *(17)* serving–creature.   115

PETER Then will I lay the serving-creature's dagger on your *(18)* pate. I

will carry no *(19)* crotchets:

I'll *re* you, I'll *fa* you; do you *(20)* note me?

1 MUSICIAN An you *re* us and *fa* us, you note us.

2 MUSICIAN Pray you, put up your dagger, and put *(21)* out your wit. 120

PETER Then have at you with my wit! I will *(22)* dry-beat you with an

1 foolish

2 laughs at your tears

   because she is in heaven

3 for the feast

4 function

5 musical (instruments)

6 mournful funeral songs

7 look with anger

8 do not provoke any more

   anger by defying them. It

   is IRONIC because what

   he really wants is Juliet

   in the vault as soon as

   possible

9 pack up

10 situation

11 PUN his instrument case

   is in need of repair

12 a popular song

13 another song of the time

14 sad song

15 pay you back thoroughly

   (PUN on their profession)

16 jeer

17 i.e. a low menial servant

18 head

19 will not tolerate your

   insults

20 PUN on previous musical

   notes

21 display

22 beat you without drawing

   blood

iron wit, and put up my iron dagger. – Answer me like men:

(1) When griping grief the heart doth wound,
And doleful (2) dumps the mind oppress,
Then music with her silver sound –   125

why *silver sound?* why *music with her silver sound?* What say
you, Simon (3) Catling?
1 MUSICIAN Marry, sir, because silver hath a sweet sound.
PETER Pretty! – What say you, Hugh (4) Rebeck?
2 MUSICIAN I say *silver sound* because musicians (5) sound for silver.   130
PETER Pretty too! – What say you, James (6) Sound-post?
3 MUSICIAN Faith, I know not what to say.
PETER O, (7) I cry you mercy; you are the singer:
(8) I will say for you. *It is music with her silver sound* because
musicians have no gold for (9) sounding: –   135

Then music with her silver sound
With speedy help doth (10) lend redress.
                                                    (Exit.
1 MUSICIAN What a (11) pestilent knave is this same!
2 MUSICIAN Hang him, (12) Jack! – Come, we'll in here; (13) tarry for the
    mourners, and stay dinner.   (Exeunt.   140

1	a further Elizabethan song
2	sorrows
3	the term for a lute string (All the musicians' names suggest musical instruments.)
4	name for a three-stringed fiddle
5	play
6	part of the structure of a violin
7	I beg your pardon
8	because he is shy
9	playing
10	make up for it (the non-payment because the feast is cancelled)
11	derisive adjective
12	for a rascal
13	wait

ACT FIVE, SCENE ONE
MANTUA – A STREET.

Enter ROMEO.

ROMEO If I may (14) trust the flattering eye of sleep,
    My dreams (15) presage some joyful news at hand:
    My (16) bosom's lord sits lightly in his throne;
    And all this day an unaccustom'd spirit
    Lifts me above the ground with cheerful thoughts.   5
    I dreamt my lady came and found me dead, –
    Strange dream, that gives a dead man (17) leave to think! –
    And breath'd such life with kisses in my lips,
    That I reviv'd, and was an emperor.
    Ah me! how sweet is (18) love itself possess'd,   10

14	believe dreams which might be true
15	pre-tell, forecast (IRONY - the news to come is death to him)
16	love in his heart
17	permission
18	the reality of love

When but love's [1] shadows are so rich in joy!

Enter BALTHASAR.

News from Verona! – How now, Balthasar!

Dost thou not bring me letters from the friar?

How doth my lady? [2] Is my father well?

How fares my Juliet? that I ask again;   15

For nothing can be ill if she be well.

BALTHASAR Then she is well, and nothing, can be ill:

Her body sleeps in Capels' [3] monument,

And her [4] immortal part with angels lives.

I saw her laid low in her kindred's vault,   20

And presently took [5] post to tell it you:

O pardon me for bringing these ill news,

Since you did leave it for my [6] office, sir.

ROMEO Is it even so? then I defy you, stars! –

Thou know'st my lodging: get me [7] ink and paper,   25

And hire post-horses; I will hence to-night.

BALTHASAR I do beseech you, sir, have patience:

Your looks are pale and wild, and do [8] import

Some [9] misadventure.

ROMEO   Tush, thou art deceiv'd: 30

Leave me, and do the thing I bid thee do.

Hast thou no letters to me from the friar?

BALTHASAR No, my good lord.

ROMEO   No matter: get thee gone,

And hire those horses; I'll be with thee [10] straight. 35

                              (*Exit* BALTHASAR.

Well, Juliet, I will lie with thee to-night.

Let's see for [11] means: – O [12] mischief, thou art swift

To enter in the thoughts of desperate men!

I do remember an [13] apothecary, –

And hereabouts he dwells, – which [14] late I noted   40

In [15] tatter'd weeds, with overwhelming brows,

[16] Culling of simples; [17] meagre were his looks,

Sharp misery had worn him to the bones:

And in his [18] needy shop a tortoise hung,

An [19] alligator stuff'd, and other skins   45

Of ill-shap'd fishes; and about his shelves

A [20] beggarly account of empty boxes,

Green earthen pots, [21] bladders, and musty seeds,

Remnants of [22] packthread, and [23] old cakes of roses,

1	the dreams of love
2	He is a dutiful son asking about his father. The IRONY is that his mother has died from the shock of his banishment
3	sepulchre IRONICALLY of course, she is not dead, the news is tragically false
4	soul
5	a swift horse
6	my job
7	to write a letter
8	suggest
9	rash happening
10	at once
11	(of killing himself)
12	evil
13	a man who sells medicines and drugs
14	I recently noticed
15	poor-looking clothes
16	sorting out herbs
17	poor
18	sparsely stocked
19	all of these were familiar items in an apothecary's shop
20	wretched number
21	containers
22	strong thread
23	perfumes

Were thinly scatter'd, to make up a show.   50
Noting this *(1)* penury, to myself I said,   1   poverty
And if a man did need a poison now,
Whose sale is *(2)* present death in Mantua,   2   the death penalty for
Here lives a *(3)* caitiff wretch would sell it him.   possessing it
O, this same thought did but *(4)* forerun my need;   55   3   miserable
And this same needy man must sell it me.   4   come before
As I remember, this should be the house:
Being holiday, the beggar's shop is shut. –
What ho! apothecary!

Enter APOTHECARY.
APOTHECARY   Who calls so loud?   60
ROMEO Come hither, man. – I see that thou art poor;
    Hold, there is forty *(5)* ducats: let me have   5   gold coins
    A dram of poison; such *(6)* soon-speeding gear   6   which is fast-acting
    As will disperse itself through all the veins,
    That the life-weary taker may fall dead;   65
    And that the *(7)* trunk may be discharg'd of breath   7   body - the GUNPOWDER
    As violently as hasty powder fir'd   image recurs
    Doth hurry from the fatal cannon's *(8)* womb.   8   interior
APOTHECARY Such *(9)* mortal drugs I have; but Mantua's   9   fatal
    Law is death to any he that *(10)* utters them.   70   10 circulates
ROMEO Art thou so *(11)* bare and full of wretchedness,   11 poor
    And fear'st to die? famine is in thy cheeks,
    Need and oppression *(12)* starveth in thine eyes,   12 you can be seen to be
    (13) Contempt and beggary hangs upon thy back,   starving
    The world is not thy friend, nor the world's law: 75   13 i.e. from others
    The world affords no law to make thee rich;
    Then be not poor, but break *(14)* it, and take this.   14 i.e. the law
APOTHECARY My poverty, but not my will consents.
ROMEO I pay thy poverty, and not thy will.
APOTHECARY Put this in any liquid thing you will,   80
    And drink it off; and, if you had the strength
    Of twenty men, it would *(15)* despatch you straight.   15 kill you immediately
ROMEO There is thy gold: worse poison to men's souls,
    Doing more murders in this loathsome world
    Than these poor *(16)* compounds that thou mayst not sell: 85   16 mixtures
    I sell thee poison, thou hast sold me none.
    Farewell: buy food, and *(17)* get thyself in flesh. –   17 fatten up
    Come, *(18)* cordial, and not poison, go with me   18 medicine
    To Juliet's grave; for there must I use thee.   *(Exeunt.*

ACT FIVE, SCENE TWO
FRIAR LAWRENCE'S CELL.

Enter FRIAR JOHN.

FRIAR JOHN Holy Franciscan friar! brother, ho!

    Enter FRIAR LAWRENCE.

FRIAR LAWRENCE This same should be the voice of Friar John.
    Welcome from Mantua: what says Romeo?
    Or, if his mind be writ, give me his letter.

FRIAR JOHN Going to find a *(1)* barefoot brother out,   5
    One of our order, to *(2)* associate me,
    Here in this city visiting the sick,
    And finding him, the *(3)* searchers of the town,
    Suspecting that we both were in a house
    Where the *(4)* infectious pestilence did reign,   10
    (5) Seal'd up the doors, and would not let us forth;
    So that my speed to Mantua there was *(6)* stay'd.

FRIAR LAWRENCE Who bare my letter, then, to Romeo?

FRIAR JOHN I could not send it, – here it is again, –
    Nor get a messenger to bring it thee,   15
    So *(7)* fearful were they of infection.

FRIAR LAWRENCE Unhappy fortune! by my *(8)* brotherhood,
    The letter was not *(9)* nice, but full of charge
    Of *(10)* dear import; and the neglecting it
    May do much danger. Friar John, go hence;   20
    Get me an iron *(11)* crow, and bring it straight
    Unto my cell.

FRIAR JOHN   Brother, I'll go and bring it thee.   *(Exit.*

FRIAR LAWRENCE Now must I to the monument alone,
    Within this three hours will fair Juliet wake: 25
    She will *(12)* beshrew me much that Romeo
    Hath had no notice of these *(13)* accidents;
    But I will write again to Mantua,
    And keep her at my cell till Romeo come; –
    Poor living corse, clos'd in a dead man's tomb!   *(Exit.* 30

1	a friar
2	keep me company
3	i.e. searching out plague victims
4	the plague
5	bolted them in to prevent the spread of infection
6	impeded
7	afraid
8	of Franciscans
9	trivial
10	very important
11	crowbar
12	curse
13	happenings (N.B. the tragedy lies in this)

ACT FIVE SCENE THREE
A CHURCHYARD; IN IT A MONUMENT BELONGING TO THE CAPULETS.

Enter ⁽¹⁾ PARIS, and his Page bearing flowers and a torch.

PARIS Give me thy torch, boy: hence, and stand ⁽²⁾ aloof; –
    Yet put it out, for I would not be seen.
    Under yond yew trees ⁽³⁾ lay thee all along,
    Holding thine ear close the hollow ground;
    So shall no foot upon the churchyard tread, –   5
    Being loose, unfirm, with digging up of graves, –
    But thou shalt hear it: whistle then to me,
    As signal that thou hear'st something approach.
    Give me those flowers. Do as I bid thee, go.
PAGE *(Aside.)* I am almost afraid to ⁽⁴⁾ stand alone   10
    Here in the churchyard; yet will I ⁽⁵⁾ adventure.   *(Retires.*
PARIS Sweet ⁽⁶⁾ flower, with flowers thy bridal bed I strew:
    O woe, thy ⁽⁷⁾ canopy is dust and stones!
    Which with ⁽⁸⁾ sweet water nightly I will dew;
    Or ⁽⁹⁾ wanting that, with tears distill'd by moans: 15
    The ⁽¹⁰⁾ obsequies that I for thee will keep,
    Nightly shall be to strew thy grave and weep.
                         (The Page *whistles.*
    The boy gives warning something doth approach.
    What cursed foot wanders this way to-night,
    To ⁽¹¹⁾ cross my obsequies and true love's ⁽¹²⁾ rite?   20
    What, with a torch! – ⁽¹³⁾ muffle me, night, awhile.   *(Retires.*

Enter ROMEO *and* BALTHASAR, *with a torch, mattock, & c.*
ROMEO Give me that ⁽¹⁴⁾ mattock and the wrenching iron.
    ⁽¹⁵⁾ Hold, take this letter; early in the morning
    See thou deliver it to my lord and father.
    Give me the light: upon thy life I charge thee,   25
    What'e'er thou hear'st or seest, stand ⁽¹⁶⁾ all aloof,
    And do not interrupt me in my course.
    Why I descend into this bed of death
    Is partly to behold my lady's face,
    But chiefly to take thence from her dead finger   30
    A precious ring, – a ring that I must use
    In ⁽¹⁷⁾ dear employment: therefore hence, be gone: –
    But if thou, ⁽¹⁸⁾ jealous, dost return to pry
    In what I further shall intend to do,

---

1 It is pure CHANCE that Paris is there at the same time as Romeo.

2 apart, well off

3 i.e. flat (in order to listen)

5

4 stay

5 risk it

6 i.e. Juliet (N.B. DEATH AS A LOVER)

7 covering

8 perfumed

15   9 lacking

10 funeral rites

20   11 disturb

12 ritual

13 hide

14 tool like a crowbar, for breaking stone

15 wait

16 well apart

17 important (he is lying to cover up his real intentions)

18 suspicious

By heaven, I will tear thee joint by joint,   35
And (1) strew this hungry churchyard with thy limbs: *1 scatter*
The time and my intents are savage-wild;
More fierce and more (2) inexorable far   *2 not to be opposed*
Than (3) empty tigers or the roaring sea.   *3 hungry*
BALTHASAR I will be gone, sir, and not trouble you.   40
ROMEO So shalt thou show me friendship. –
(4) Take thou that: *4 he gives him money*
Live and (5) be prosperous: and farewell, good fellow.   *5 the gift was obviously*
BALTHASAR For all this same, I'll hide me here-about: *very generous*
His looks I fear, and his (6) intents I doubt.   *(Retires.*   45   *6 I am afraid of his*
ROMEO Thou detestable (7) maw, thou womb of death,   *intentions*
Gorg'd with the (8) dearest morsel of the earth,   *7 stomach (i.e. the grave)*
Thus I enforce thy rotten jaws to open,   *8 Juliet (he continues the*
            (Breaking open the door of the monument.   *image of the stomach*
And, in (9) despite, I'll cram thee with more food!   *gorging food)*
PARIS This is that banish'd (10) haughty Montague   50   *9 in defiance*
That murder'd my love's cousin, – (11) with which grief,   *10 high-handed*
It is supposed, the fair creature died, –   *11 IRONIC because he has*
And here is come to do some (12) villanous shame   *the wrong facts*
To the dead bodies: I will apprehend him. –   *(Advances.*   *12 desecration*
Stop thy (13) unhallow'd toil, vile Montague!   55   *13 unholy*
Can vengeance by pursu'd further than death?
Condemned villain, I do (14) apprehend thee: *14 arrest*
Obey, and go with me; for thou must die.
ROMEO (15) I must indeed; and therefore came I hither. –   *15 Paris cannot possibly*
(16) Good gentle youth, tempt not a desperate man;   60   *understand this, IRONIC*
Fly hence, and leave me: – think upon these (17) gone;   *answer*
Let them affright thee. – I beseech thee, youth,   *16 he fails to recognize Paris*
Put not (18) another sin upon my head   *17 corpses in the grave*
By urging me to fury. O, be gone!   *18 to add to murder and*
By heaven, I love thee better than myself;   65   *suicide*
For I come hither arm'd (19) against myself: *19 i.e. with the poison bottle*
Stay not, be gone; – live, and hereafter say,
A madman's mercy bade thee run away.
PARIS I do defy thy (20) conjurations,   *20 what you have bade me*
And (21) apprehend thee for a felon here.   70   *to do*
ROMEO Wilt thou provoke me? then have at thee, boy!   *(They fight.*   *21 arrest you as a criminal*
PAGE O lord, they fight! I will go call the watch.   *(Exit.*
PARIS O, I am slain! *(Falls.)* – If thou be merciful,
Open the tomb, lay me with Juliet.   *(Dies.*
ROMEO In faith, I will. – Let me (22) peruse this face: –   75   *22 look upon*

Mercutio's kinsman, noble County Paris! –
What said my man, when my *(1)* betossed soul | *1* tossed about by distress
Did not attend him as we rode? I think
He told me Paris should have married Juliet:
Said he not so? or did I dream it so?   80
Or am I mad, hearing him talk of Juliet,
To think it was so? – O, give me thy hand,
One writ *(2)* with me in sour misfortune's book! | *2* their names will be
I'll bury thee in a *(3)* triumphant grave; – | together in the book of
A grave? O no, a *(4)* lantern, slaughter'd youth,   85 | bad luck
For here lies Juliet, and her beauty makes | *3* glorious
This vault a *(5)* feasting presence full of light. | *4* lighted dome
Death, lie thou there, by a *(6)* dead man interr'd. | *5* a banqueting hall (which
(Laying PARIS *in the monument.* | would be well-lit)
How oft when men are at the point of death | *6* his intended suicide
Have they been merry! which their *(7)* keepers call   90 | *7* gaolers
A lightning before death: O, how may I
Call this a lightning? – O my love! my wife!
Death, that hath suck'd the honey of thy breath,
Hath had no power yet upon thy beauty:
Thou art not conquer'd; beauty's *(8)* ensign yet   95 | *8* Flag - DRAMATIC IRONY
Is crimson in thy lips and in thy cheeks, | - she has colour in her
And death's pale flag is not advanced there. – | cheeks because she is
Tybalt, liest thou there in thy *(9)* bloody sheet? | reviving from the drug
O, what more favour can I do to thee | *9* shroud - burial cloth
Than with that hand that cut thy youth in twain   100
To sunder *(10)* his that was thine enemy? | *10* i.e. to take his own life
Forgive me, *(11)* cousin! – Ah, dear Juliet, | *11* he is speaking as Juliet's
Why art thou yet so fair? Shall I believe | husband
That *(12)* unsubstantial death is amorous; | *12* without substance, a
And that the lean abhorred monster keeps   105 | body
Thee here in dark to be his *(13)* paramour? | *13* LOVER
For fear of that I still will stay with thee,
And never from this palace *(14)* of dim night | *14* associated with the dark
Depart again: here, here will I remain
With worms that are thy chambermaids; O, here   110
Will I set up my everlasting rest;
And *(15)* shake the yoke of inauspicious stars | *15* cast off the burden of bad
From this world-wearied flesh. – Eyes, look your last! | luck from my world -
Arms, take your last embrace! and, lips, O you | weary body
The doors of breath, *(16)* seal with a righteous kiss   115 | *16* sign, as on a document
A *(17)* dateless bargain to engrossing death! – | *17* an eternal agreement

Come, bitter *(1)* conduct, come, unsavoury guide!
Thou desperate *(2)* pilot, now at once run on
The dashing rocks thy sea-sick weary *(3)* bark!
Here's to my love! *(Drinks.)* – O true apothecary!   120
Thy drugs are *(4)* quick. – Thus with a kiss I die.   *(Dies.*

Enter, at the other end of the Churchyard, FRIAR LAWRENCE, *with
a lantern, crow, and spade.*

FRIAR LAWRENCE Saint Francis *(5)* be my speed! how oft to-night
Have my old feet *(6)* stumbled at graves! – Who's there?
Who is it that *(7)* consorts, so late, the dead?

BALTHASAR Here's one, a friend, and one that knows you well.   125

FRIAR LAWRENCE *(8)* Bliss be upon you! Tell me, good my friend,
What torch is yond that *(9)* vainly lends his light
To grubs and eyeless sculls? as I discern,
It burneth in the Capels' monument.

BALTHASAR It doth so, holy sir; and there's my master,   130
One that you love.

FRIAR LAWRENCE   Who is it?

BALTHASAR   Romeo.

FRIAR LAWRENCE How long hath he been there?

BALTHASAR   Full half an hour.   135

FRIAR LAWRENCE Go with me to the vault.

BALTHASAR   I dare not, sir:
My master knows not but I am gone hence;
And fearfully did *(10)* menace me with death
If I did stay to look on his *(11)* intents.   140

FRIAR LAWRENCE Stay, then; I'll go alone: – fear comes upon me;
O, much I fear some ill unlucky thing.

BALTHASAR *(12)* As I did sleep under this yew tree here,
I dreamt my master and another fought,
And that my master slew him.   145

FRIAR LAWRENCE   Romeo!   *(Advances.*
Alack, alack, what blood is this which stains
The stony entrance of this sepulchre? –
What mean these *(13)* masterless and gory swords
To lie discolour'd by this place of peace?   150
                    (Enters the monument.
Romeo! O, pale! – Who else? what, Paris too?
And *(14)* steep'd in blood? – Ah, what an *(15)* unkind hour
Is guilty of this lamentable chance! –
The lady stirs.   *(*JULIET *wakes and stirs.*

1 conductor (i.e. the poison conducted through his body)
2 i.e. himself. This is the third time the PILOT image is used
3 ship (himself)
4 Even at his death, Romeo PUNS - quick means "alive".
5 help me to be quick
6 stumbling was superstitiously seen as a bad omen
7 keeps company with
8 happiness
9 in vain
10 threaten
11 plans
12 He is not telling the truth, possibly to protect Romeo.
13 bloodstained swords which have been left there
14 soaked
15 unnatural. It is CHANCE that he is literally minutes too late.

JULIET O *(1)* comfortable friar! where is my lord? –   155   *1 bringing comfort*
    I do remember well where I should be,
    And there I am: – where is my Romeo?

                          (Noise within.

FRIAR LAWRENCE I hear some noise. – Lady, come from that nest
    Of death, *(2)* contagion, and unnatural sleep: *2 infection*
    A greater power than we can *(3)* contradict   160   *3 defy*
    Hath *(4)* thwarted our intents: – Come, come away: *4 destroyed our plans*
    Thy husband in thy bosom there lies dead;
    And Paris too: – come, I'll dispose of thee
    Among a sisterhood of holy nuns:
    Stay not to question, for the watch is coming;   165
    Come, go, good Juliet *(noise again),* – I dare no longer stay.
JULIET Go, get thee hence, for I will not away. –

                    (Exit FRIAR LAWRENCE.

    What's here? a cup, clos'd in my true love's hand?
    Poison, I see, hath been his *(5)* timeless end: –   *5 untimely*
    O churl! drink all, and leave no friendly drop   170
    To help me after? – I will kiss thy lips;   *6 perhaps*
    (6) Haply some poison yet doth hang on them,   *7 the kiss she places on his*
    To make me die with a *(7)* restorative.   *(Kisses him.*   *lips*
    (8) Thy lips are warm!   *8 IRONY in that she also*
1 WATCH *(Within.)* Lead, boy: – which way?   175   *was just too late*
JULIET Yea, noise? – then I'll be brief. – O *(9)* happy dagger!   *9 fortunate that she has*
                (Snatching ROMEO'S *dagger.*   *found it*
    This is thy *(10)* sheath *(stabs herself);* there rest, and let me die.   *10 i.e. her breast*
             (Falls on ROMEO'S *body, and dies.*

    Enter Watch, *with the Page of* PARIS.
PAGE This is the place; there, where the torch doth burn.
1 WATCH The ground is bloody; search about the churchyard:
    Go some of you, whoe'er you find *(11)* attach.   180   *11 arrest*
               (Exeunt some of the Watch.
    Pitiful sight! here lies the county slain; –
    And Juliet bleeding; warm, and newly dead,
    Who here hath lain these *(12)* two days buried. –   *12 (inaccuracy in time here)*
    Go, tell the prince, – run to the Capulets, –
    Raise up the Montagues, – some others search: 185
               (Exeunt other of the Watch.
    We see the ground whereon these woes do lie;   *13 reason*
    But the true *(13)* ground of all these piteous woes   *14 without knowing the*
    We cannot *(14)* without circumstance descry.   *circumstances*

Re-enter some of the Watch *with* Balthasar.
2 Watch Here's Romeo's man; we found him in the churchyard.
1 Watch Hold him in safety till the prince come hither.   190

Re-enter others of the Watch *with* Friar Lawrence.
3 Watch Here is a friar, that trembles, sighs, and weeps:
    We took this mattock and this spade from him
    As he was coming from this churchyard *(1)* side.
1 Watch A great suspicion: *(2)* stay the friar too.

Enter the Prince *and* Attendants.
Prince What misadventure is so early up,   195
    That calls our person from our morning's rest?

Enter Capulet, Lady Capulet, *and others.*
Capulet What should it be, that they so shriek abroad?
Lady Capulet The people in the street cry Romeo,
    Some Juliet, and some Paris; and all run,
    With open outcry, toward our monument.   200
Prince What fear is this which startles *(3)* in our ears?
1 Watch Sovereign, here lies the County
    Paris slain;
    And Romeo dead; and Juliet, dead before,
    Warm and new kill'd.   205
Prince Search, seek, and know how this foul murder comes.
1 Watch Here is a friar, and slaughter'd Romeo's man,
    With instruments upon them fit to open
    These dead men's tombs.
Capulet O heaven! – O wife, look how our daughter bleeds!   210
    This dagger hath *(4)* mista'en, – for, lo, his house
    Is *(5)* empty on the back of Montague, –
    And is mid-sheathed in my daughter's bosom!
Lady Capulet O me! this sight of death is as a bell
    That warns my *(6)* old age to a sepulchre.   215

Enter Montague *and others.*
Prince Come, Montague; for thou art early up,
    To see thy son and heir more *(7)* early down.
Montague Alas, my liege, my wife is dead to-night;
    Grief of my son's exile hath stopp'd her breath:
    What further woe conspires against my age?   220
Prince Look, and thou shalt see.

1   the side of the church (It is rather disappointing that the Friar appears to be running away!)

2   hold

3   this could mean, "is shocking to our ears"

4   is in the wrong place

5   it should be in the sheath belonging to Romeo

6   (Lady Capulet is not old, she is 28. The IRONY is that she feels aged with the shock)

7   dead so young

MONTAGUE O thou *(1)* untaught! what manners is in this.   *1*   Ill-mannered, to go

    To press before thy father to a grave?   before your father to the

PRINCE *(2)* Seal up the mouth of outrage for awhile,   grave

    Till we can clear these *(3)* ambiguities,   225   *2*   Hold your cries of grief

    And know their *(4)* spring, their head, their true descent;   *3*   confusions

    And then will I be *(5)* general of your woes,   *4*   origin

    And lead you even to *(6)* death: meantime forbear,   *5*   leader

    And let *(7)* mischance be slave to patience. –   *6*   almost to dying

    Bring forth the parties of suspicion.   230   *7*   unlucky happenings be

FRIAR LAWRENCE I am the *(8)* greatest, able to do least,   overcome by calmness

    Yet most suspected, as the time and place   *8*   i.e. the prime suspect

    Doth *(9)* make against me, of this direful murder;   *9*   conspire against

    And here I stand, both to *(10)* impeach and purge   *10* accuse and clear

    Myself condemned and myself excus'd.   235

PRINCE Then say at once what thou dost know in this.

FRIAR LAWRENCE I will be brief, for my *(11)* short date of breath   *11* life line

    Is not so long as is a tedious tale.

    Romeo, there dead, was husband to that Juliet;

    And she, there dead, that Romeo's faithful wife: 240

    I married them; and their *(12)* stol'n marriage-day   *12* secret

    Was Tybalt's *(13)* doomsday, whose untimely death   *13* the day he died

    Banish'd a new-made bridegroom from this city;

    For whom, and not for Tybalt, Juliet pin'd.

    You, to remove that *(14)* siege of grief from her,   245   *14* attack (N.B. the

    Betroth'd, and would have married her *(15)* perforce,   MILITARY metaphor)

    To County Paris: – then comes she to me,   *15* coerced her

    And, with wild looks, bid me devise some means

    To rid her from this second marriage,

    Or in my cell there would she kill herself.   250

    Then gave I her, so tutor'd by my art,

    A sleeping potion; which so took effect

    As I intended, for it *(16)* wrought on her   *16* brought about

    The form of death: meantime I writ to Romeo

    That he should hither come as this *(17)* dire night,   255   *17* dreadful

    To help to take her from her borrow'd grave,

    Being the time the potion's force should cease,

    But he which bore my letter, Friar John,

    Was stay'd by accident; and yesternight

    Return'd my letter back. Then all alone   260

    At the *(18)* prefixed hour of her waking   *18* pre-arranged

    Came I to take her from her kindred's vault;

    Meaning to keep her *(19)* closely at my cell   *19* secretly

Till I conveniently could send to Romeo:
But when I came, – some minute ere the time   265
Of her awaking, – here untimely lay
The noble Paris and true Romeo dead.
She wakes; and I entreated her come forth,
And bear this work of heaven with patience:
But then a noise did scare me from the tomb;   270
And she, too desperate, would not go with me,
But, as it seems, did violence on herself.
All this I know; and to the marriage
Her nurse is *(1)* privy: and if ought in this   *1* party to (these secrets)
Miscarried by my fault, let my old life   275
Be sacrific'd, some hour before his time,
Unto the rigour of severest law.

PRINCE We still have known thee for a holy man. –
    Where's Romeo's man? what can he say in this?

BALTHASAR I brought my master news of Juliet's death;   280
    And then *(2)* in post he came from Mantua   *2* in haste
    To this same place, to this same monument.
    This letter he early bid me give his father;
    And threaten'd me with death, going in the vault,
    If I departed not, and left him there.   285

PRINCE Give me the letter, – I will look on it. –
    Where is the county's page that rais'd the watch? –
    Sirrah, what made your master in this place?

PAGE He came with flowers to strew his lady's grave;
    And bid me stand *(3)* aloof, and so I did: 290   *3* apart
    (4) Anon comes one with light to ope the tomb;   *4* immediately
    And by and by my master drew on him;
    And then I ran away to call the watch.

PRINCE This letter doth make good the friar's words,
    Their course of love, the tidings of her death: 295
    And here he writes that he did buy a poison
    Of a poor 'pothecary, and *(5)* therewithal   *5* with that
    Come to this vault to die, and lie with Juliet. –   *6* enmity
    Where be these enemies? – Capulet, and Montague, –   *7* your children have been
    See what a scourge is laid upon your *(6)* hate,   300   killed by love (N.B. the
    That heaven finds means to kill your joys with *(7)* love!   ANTITHESIS)
    And I, for *(8)* winking at your discords too,   *8* shutting my eyes to
    Have lost a *(9)* brace of kinsmen: – all are punish'd.   *9* a pair (Mercutio and

CAPULET O brother Montague, give me thy hand: Paris)
    This is my daughter's *(10)* jointure, for no more   305   *10* marriage settlement

Can I demand.
MONTAGUE   But I can give thee more:
For I will raise her statue in pure gold;
That while Verona by that name is known,
There shall no figure at such *(1)* rate be set   310 | *1* shall be of such value
As that of true and faithful Juliet.
CAPULET As rich shall Romeo by his lady lie;
Poor sacrifices of our enmity!
PRINCE A *(2)* glooming peace this morning with it brings; | *2* dark
The sun *(3)* for sorrow will not show his head: 315 | *3* for sadness
Go hence, to have more talk of these sad things;
Some shall be pardon'd and some punish'd:
For never was a story of more woe
Than this of Juliet and her Romeo.   *(Exeunt.*